QUIET
DESPERATION

QUIET DESPERATION

A NOVELLA

RODNEY NELSESTUEN

atmosphere press

Chapter 1

Chicago, Illinois. Friday, May 3, 1996.

"You wanted to see me?" Jerry says. I look up into the face of my law partner, the same face I've seen for fifteen years, unchanged in all that time. The narrow head, sharply defined nose and thin lips beneath high, pale cheekbones all converge to make him seem a mere boy or a demon, but the latter depends on which side of an issue you find yourself. Jerry has a slight build that makes him look shorter than he is. Still, an observer might think him an athlete. The shiny black suit matches hair that starts low on his forehead. It's been gelled to a shine with comb streaks pulling it back over his head in a slight wave. The natural curl takes over wave by wave throughout the day until, by five o'clock, it regains the full-bodied attraction, the handsome, aw-shucks-good-guy look he works to overcome. It's still before noon, so he remains the fierce lawyer, sleekened to a razor's edge.

"Yes, yes, I did," I say. "Jerry, we've got a great new opportunity. Lots of exposure on this one, both good and bad." I hand him the only file on my desk. He sets it in his lap and crosses his legs, waits. I know he's stressing over the fact that I know something he doesn't. I hide my amusement. "Well, you'll never guess who came in to see me this morning."

"No, I'll probably never guess," he replies.

He's off his game today. Normally, he'd engage Margaret as he passed by her desk to gain at least a clue what this could

3

be about. "Well, I'll get to the point," I say. "Samuel Armstor was here and wants us to represent him."

"Armstor?"

"Watch the news? Controller at RoneCraft? Same guy you could have seen being cuffed in the company parking lot and stuffed in the back seat of a federal limo—if you'd watched the late news last night."

Jerry's head turns slightly and his eyes follow, like a compass pulled seventeen degrees off magnetic north. Normally, he faces down his prey, eyes studying me, working out what it would take to destroy me. This is good, I think, even-steven so far. But the day is young, and I have few illusions about my ability to stand toe-to-toe with Jerry. He nods. "I didn't, but I saw it online this morning. Yes, Armstor, that's the name," he says, as if he'd remembered it all by himself.

"Well," I say, "we're going to represent him on the accounting fraud charges."

Jerry puts his elbows on the armrests, raises his hands and presses his fingertips together in that classic pose. His hands are large and friendly, disarming if you don't know him. He uses the pose to mask whatever he's feeling at the moment. It's confusing now since he waits for me to go on, but it's his turn now, his ball, his serve. I feel my father looking down on us from the mahogany-framed portrait behind my desk— keeping score. I'm not breathing and don't really know why. Ridiculous... nonsense...

I wait him out.

Jerry finally responds, "This is good news, Winston, if we handle it right." His eyes scan my desk. He holds up the file. "This all you got?"

"Well, we just met this morning. He didn't bring much with him. It was our first meeting."

"Did he... cook the books?"

"I didn't get that far—well, he did say the accounting was wrong. He was sizing us up, really. He just wanted to see what we could do for him."

"So, he's not really our client?"

"No, I mean, yes, he is. He said he wants us to represent him, definitely. Look, here's his side of the story: he was responsible for the company books. I didn't get all of it, but it had something to do with accounting for goodwill from a series of acquisitions: that and some off-balance sheet partnerships. Jesus, Jerry, you know I don't have a handle on this accounting stuff. Anyway..."

"He says he just did what he was told to do, right?"

"Right." I look at the humidor on my desk. The table has turned in just a few words. I used to watch my father at times like this. He'd slow down and open the humidor, take out a cigar, spin it deliberately in his fingers and moisten the end, turning it in his lips, a thoughtful knit to his brow. When I was a boy, I thought it fascinating to watch if, I dared watch. By the time I went to college, I saw the fondled cigar as merely phallic.

"What else did he tell you?"

"What I said... what you already know... that he was charged with falsifying financial records, and that includes SEC reports, and *that* makes it a federal offense, and *that's* why the goddamn feds arrested him."

"Why did he come to us?"

"Because they all come to us. Because we're so damned... because *you* are so damned good at getting these guys off."

"Did Ellen sit in?"

"No, Armstor said he wanted to see me alone."

Jerry nods, looks away and taps his fingers together again. "Get a retainer?"

"Twenty thousand."

"Good grief, Winston, that won't buy lunch for the battalion of CPAs we're going to need."

"It's all he could get free. Hell, most of his assets were probably frozen before they picked him up."

"But he's smart enough, I assume. What about his house?

Is it in his wife's name?"

"I don't know." I splay my hands. "Should have thought of that."

"Never mind. I'll call the real estate group, and they can locate his address and the legal description. We better move fast because whatever equity they have in it will be gone soon, and there might be other creditors—not to mention the stockholder lawsuits that will start to line up."

Jerry will reach in on anything I'm doing, snatch it from me like a harried mother pulling sharp scissors from the hand of her two-year-old, then sighing at the burden of responsibility. Part of me is relieved. Another part hates him for it since it's altogether too much like my father's habit—back when he was functional, that is.

"And you get Armstor back here by four thirty today. Tell him it's imperative. I'll sit in, and Ellen, too," Jerry says.

Ellen. My face must be answering him without my knowing. "Look, we need her, Winston. She's damned good in corporate law and a top-notch CPA in her own right. You should have had her sit in. Hell, you said yourself you didn't understand everything he told you about the accounting."

Ellen is one person I never enjoy seeing. But I can't worry about her right now. Besides, at this point, I don't know why he even wants me at the meeting. "It's Friday," I say. "I need to leave by five thirty." Now Jerry can't look at me. He knows about Paula.

"What about Shirley? Thought she had chemo today."

"Shirley's with her sister. She'll be fine."

I stare at him now. I can handle this part simply because I'm not threatened by his knowledge of Paula. Jerry has his own, shall we say, ambiguities. He's never been married and doesn't date. I have never caught him looking at a woman the way I know I do. I could go on, but suffice it to say that he's gay. I called him on it, sort of, just after Dad made him a partner. By luck, I struck at a bad time. He didn't quite come all the way clean, but he did say he'd just broken up with someone. I could tell it was tough on him. When I suggested that

I knew he was talking about a man, he nodded, I think, and then left my office. It's amazing what one can learn during a wordless encounter.

I've never gotten within a mile of the topic since. But needing to define him fully, I just assume one logical reason for him: his partner may have had AIDS. Or Jerry, always a man of discipline and caution, may just have decided to go life alone for the time being. At any rate, he's likely not one to come out of the closet. I don't know where he finds his relationships, and it seems no one else in Chicago, at least among our mutual acquaintances, knows either. Those of us closest to him all seem to share the understanding that he's gay. We've no proof, never speak of it, but it's there as fact just the same.

He's probably the most conservative man I know—politically speaking, that is; and he's been known to turn down cases, or rather refer them to one of our staff attorneys, where sexual impropriety will be the central theme. Taken together, Jerry seems an odd amalgamation of opposing characters and mores. At the same time, he's one of the most normal people I know, a guy, a regular guy, adding to my reasons for hating him.

Jerry puts his hands on the arms of the chair. "Anything else?" he asks. The pause before standing tells me the answer he wants.

"No, no."

He stands. "Good, then. I'll see you at four thirty. And I'll bring Ellen and the mortgage papers. We can still get them recorded before the Registrar's office closes."

I look at my watch. It's now eleven fifteen. The hollow question mark returns, this time deep in my bowels. I can't let it take me into that state of depression, the inability to move or think, as it did this morning. But the only source of relief is about to leave my office.

"Jerry..."

"Yes?"

"You free for lunch?"

He looks toward the door. "No, afraid not. Like you said, it's Friday." He smiles. "Your father's coming. You know what he says every Friday—'Just checking on my pension.'" He leaves.

I close my eyes and can see my father's wheelchair in the foyer as it is every Friday. But I can't think about him now because exhaustion rolls over me. It comes in waves that crash against me, eroding the shoreline of my self-esteem, nibbling at who I am. It seems dramatic, I know, but yesterday, I had the revelation that it isn't new. It's been there for more than thirty years—at first, nothing more than small breakers nudging me. But they grew to sizable waves through the years. Then, not too long ago, I noticed they'd changed, grown to monsters that pound and retreat, landing hard and dragging a part of me out to sea in their retreat. There are days I fear a final tsunami will come to finish the job, and at this very moment, I half wish for it.

But I have a task now. I must find a way to call Armstor and have him return at four thirty. But why would the man listen to me? And bring his wife? No, he certainly won't come just because Winston Williamsen III asks. But then maybe... He might come, has to come. Jerry's expecting it, and Ellen will be there, and if Armstor doesn't come, then it only deepens their doubts about me. But of course, there's Margaret, my secretary of twenty-some years.

I press the intercom. "Margaret."

"Yes, Mr. Williamsen."

"You have Armstor's number?"

"Yes, sir. Do you need it?"

"No. I want you to call him. Tell him he and his wife need to get back here at four thirty today. Tell him it's important... the defense team, we need to meet with him."

"You want me to let Mr. Koch know?"

"Jerry already knows. He'll contact Ellen, but I want you to call her, too. Make sure she'll be there."

"Yes, Mr. Williamsen."

"And get my wife on the line."

"Yes, Mr. Williamsen." Margaret's voice disappears, and I know with certainty she's sprung into action. Margaret is neat, fastidious, and clean as a whistle but plain. She could be attractive if she had some guidance on using makeup. But she doesn't have the time. Her quadriplegic husband, a car accident more than a dozen years ago, is alone in their apartment, navigating the furniture in a pipette-powered wheelchair. She makes ready his every moment before coming to work, then rushes home to dote on him all evening. Through all *her* trials, she's never wavered in any part of what she does around here. I marvel, jealously, that she finds firm ground where all I see is quicksand.

But now, I can breathe again.

I've not always been like this. For most of my life, I've been an able, if average, attorney. I've worked long hours and sometimes had to run with scissors, despite the risk, to make up for my mediocrity. My father's firm is successful in almost every measure of a law firm's success. But some time ago—I no longer remember when—the pompous, self-assured, take-charge son he named as managing partner fifteen years ago, *me*, was de-fanged, de-clawed, neutered. I did it to myself... but I can't think about that now. My private line is blinking, and in a second, Margaret will tell me Shirley's on hold. I've got to handle that conversation well so I can turn my thoughts to Paula.

"Hello."

"Hello, Winston," Shirley says. "What is it you want? I'm leaving for the clinic in a couple of minutes. Carol's just going out the door to pull the car around."

"I know you don't have much time. I just wanted to see how you were."

"Tired. Same as yesterday and the day before."

"I suppose. Well, I was just checking in on you." Shirley says nothing, but I imagine her covering her eyes with one hand, waiting for a wave of exhaustion to pass for what I'll say next.

"I won't be home until late," I say, "probably after midnight. I have a client coming in at five thirty, and we're meeting for dinner, and we'll probably go over his case tonight. Then tomorrow morning, I've got to meet him at the office."

Shirley's silence tells me she's considering what I've said. Since her cancer returned, she's spent more time watching me but less asking what I might be doing. I could be telling the truth—it has been true in the past that I'd meet a client on Friday and work through the weekend to prepare for a Monday trial. But I haven't done that for over a year, although she seems to pretend I still do, even with ample evidence, circumstantial as it is, that it's another tryst.

"Big case?"

"Big enough, or routine. Nothing unusual, but we have a lot of work to do." I can't tell if she's still there or has set the receiver down as she sometimes does. "Well, don't wait up for me," I say. "I'll be there when I get there."

"Bye," she says. I don't answer because I won't get the word out before she hangs up. Besides, we're past it now, the obligatory call, checking in, telling her I'll be late. I've done what I must and wonder if, in the thousands of calls between husbands and wives each day, the numbing effect of left-over dial tone is universal.

No matter, nonsense, in fact. I've done what's expected both with Shirley and for this afternoon's meeting, where I'll sit in and be the quiet, gelded counselor that I am.

As I said, it wasn't always this way. For most of my career, I was in the battle, always up to it, year in and year out. But then along came the Molotelco case. I was the lead attorney in this obscure but serious class action suit just a few years ago. The board at Molotelco Communications agreed to retain the firm at its regular hourly rates. They said they'd double the fee if the charges of slamming and moving customers from their current provider to Molotelco without their permission were dismissed.

In the course of my work, I discovered six handwritten memos from the executive committee. They were damning and would have been a problem. It's amazing what incriminations otherwise bright people will commit to writing.

I destroyed them. It would have been all right, except a copy of two of the memos surfaced. These were the weakest evidence against my client, but they referred to the other memos, and I made the mistake of telling Jerry I'd destroyed them. Jerry, as he said, "did the right thing" and informed the court of an "inadvertent destruction of potential evidence."

He negotiated with the State Bar ethics committee during the investigation. I was only reprimanded, mainly because my then-still-cogent father made some calls. The matter was let go except for the fierce tongue lashing my father gave me in front of Shirley.

On one hand, I understood the gravity of what I'd done. On the other hand, crossing the line had paid off. After all, the case against Molotelco was dismissed, and Molotelco paid us over four million dollars, a lot of money for a firm that never takes contingency cases. Besides, I had, by then, lost confidence in my ability to win a case on its merits.

Jerry was furious and made me promise to discuss what I was thinking before ever considering that type of action again. "Ethics and the law are a high wire act," he'd said, as if talking to a first-year law student. Jerry has always been able to walk that wire with its tenuous weave of things—legal but just this side of unethical.

It was lost on me somewhere along the line—the adversarial legal system where each side fights for its own at all costs. Instead, it seems little more than a series of half-truths told as if they were all true. Truth is, it never did make sense to me in law school. But once I joined the firm, I embraced it and lived for it as a young man's first bitter taste of alcohol soon becomes addictive.

But the Molotelco case finally beat me down, and I retreated to the shadows of day-to-day management of the firm, relegated to collecting fees from deadbeat clients and attending Rotary Club meetings. Any time I come near a real case, Jerry steps in. It's already happened here, with Armstor, the thought of which makes me want to call Paula. But she's at work, folding clothes and floor walking at Nordstrom. There's nothing left but waiting for tonight.

But there is the matter of my father's noon visit. It falls to Margaret to have him fetched from his house since Shirley's cancer returned and his dependence on the wheelchair is almost complete. At eighty-six, he's slipping fast with both mind and body giving out. A series of day nurses have kept it going so far, but it's getting more difficult, and the time is near when he'll need care around the clock.

I dread each Friday and have made it a point not to let him see me in the office. The last time I did, he was in a confused state and greeted me by reliving, no, repeating the confrontation we had when I was in college:

"Well, it's about time, then," he'd said, pointing a crooked finger at me.

"What do you mean?"

*"Clear as the nose on your face, boy. You have **got** to straighten out. Stop this foolish idea of becoming a writer and focus on the **law**, son. Your mother and I won't support you **forever**, you know." His arms began to flail. He grabbed the rubber wheels on his chair and tried to draw closer, but couldn't remember how to make it move.*

"Dad, I'm not in college now. I am a lawyer, remember? I manage the firm now, your firm."

"What did you say?"

"I said you're talking about a time over thirty years ago."

*He looked down at his lap, the chair, and then around the room. His sagging face seemed to ask a question. "Well, I mean it, Winston. I've been hearing you're running around with **women** and not going to class. **Worst** of all, you're telling people you're not **going** to be a lawyer." He slapped both hands on the armrests. I was embarrassed, standing in the* *reception area with a few clients and half the staff within earshot. The more they pretended nothing unusual was happening, the worse I felt.*

I crouched beside the wheelchair to quiet him. "But I am a lawyer, Dad."

He shook his finger again. "You'll mind me now, son. You're going to take over the firm someday. Hear me?"

I gave up and put my hand on his arm. "Yes, Dad, I hear you. I will." He slumped in the chair, and we all stood by, listening to the raspy breath we all believed would someday become a death rattle.

That was his worst day so far. He seems almost normal most of the time, and sometimes I want to kneel close beside him and take his hand, get his eyes to focus on me: *Dad, it's me. It's me. Me.* But I can't. I couldn't.

I've been able to keep his affairs going and patch together a system of care without his permission, but like the shoe-maker's barefoot children, I've not taken it far enough and soon must become his *legal* guardian. He won't like it, may even fight me on it when his head's clear. But there's little choice, and it's certain the time is at hand, as certain as cancer's grip on Shirley.

And now I hear the dimmed rustle of excitement in the lobby. My father has arrived. The walnut panels of my closed door nearly hum with the timbre of his laughter. It seems out of place here, where he seldom laughed in fifty years. I look up at his portrait behind my desk. A robust man in a dark suit looks down at me. Probably in his mid-fifties when that portrait was done: wide lapels, red tie too full for today's style, and a lifetime of eating too well gave him a middle still visible in the suits tailored to hide his girth. The head well shaped, a shock of white hair combed neatly, a bit large in the forehead but exuding intelligence. It's the eyes, though, that trouble me. Every morning, I take my desk, knowing that the image he created stares down at me in judgment. I seldom study the painting like this because of those eyes, eyes that seem to change throughout the day. Of course, it is I who change. Still, this moment is one of the few I take in defiance, and I stare up at him, come what may.

But now he's retired, been relegated to the wheelchair, hair thinning fast, shoulders shrinking into his gut. He's begun to lose both memory and bladder control and, for some unknown reason, doesn't take the degradation as hard as the man I knew would have. And strange upon strange, there's been more humor in him. Oh, and the office staff loves his Friday visits.

I sneak to the door and crack it open to see him surrounded by Margaret, Ellen, and two secretaries. He seems clear-headed from where I am. I feel the pull of his laughter as if that sound alone could fill me up. I consider risking his seeing me, but hesitate as Jerry approaches from down the hall.

Dad looks up and smiles at him. "How's it going, Sonny?" he asks. "You still got all those bastards on the run?"

"Oh, you know it's not like that anymore, WW." Jerry leans over and puts one arm around him, pats him on the shoulder. I ease my door shut and turn away.

Chapter 2

At exactly four thirty-five, Margaret pulls the door of the glass conference room shut as she leaves. I sit in the dark leather chair facing the panorama of Chicago's skyline, exterior windows facing out on two sides. I imagine the buildings to the east are gone, three blocks' worth, demolished so that, in the distance, I can see Lake Michigan's shoreline running north and south from Navy Pier while its blue waters fade eastward into the sky. It's a silly thought, but one that lets me put off dealing with the moment.

Still, I'm acutely aware of the time and know I'll be pressed to end this by five thirty. No one speaks, and it's clear they await my lead, which puts me in charge, which I both like and loathe. In the silence, I feel the ticking of the grandfather clock in the foyer of my father's home. That was where, when he was angry, I'd wait on the bench beneath the antique coat tree, hearing the clock's tick and considering what punishment lay ahead. It was an eight-foot clock with a tick bold enough to punish all by itself.

Directly across from me sits Samuel Armstor and his wife, Meghan. On either end of the cherry conference table are Jerry and Ellen. We are positioned just so, the lawyer's version of seating at the last supper. We do this on purpose and have for years: *strategic seating*, my uncreative father coined it. Meetings like this have been my life's work, my stock in trade, and I could almost turn the tape on and let it play, except for the ticking clock.

I push forward. "Thank you, Sam. You, as well, Mrs. Armstor, for coming in on such short notice. As I said when I first introduced you, Jerry here will be the lead trial attorney, and Ellen will provide backup. Sam, Ellen is a certified public accountant and has extensive experience in accounting matters, especially as they've played out in some rather notable trials."

Armstor turns to Jerry. "Mr. Koch, Winston said you're top-notch."

Jerry is evaluating Samuel Armstor, but smiles and relaxes as he speaks. "Yes, well, we have experience with federal charges like those levied against you."

Jerry likes to sit to one side, watch, and say little during the first meeting. His smile warms the room while something serene rises to the surface of his face. He studies the client, who is oblivious, like a rabbit unaware that the soaring grace of the hawk overhead masks its deadly search for movement in the grass.

He wants to know how the client will fare at trial. Will he look worried or sweaty or cool or detached? Could he even *look* innocent? Or will the smallish demeanor, the classic bald head of the nondescript, stereotypical accountant, something Armstor personifies, combine with his fingers, too small and thin even for his diminished stature, to give him away? As far as I can tell, he's guilty as hell.

Armstor wants to turn toward Ellen but doesn't. An innocent man wouldn't be intimidated by another accountant. He'd see her as his best ally and hope for vindication. Jerry sees it, too. Our eyes meet, and that tells me it's time for the wingless-fly-on-the-table treatment. We let Armstor and his wife sit in total silence while we study them.

Armstor picks at the too-long nails on his fingers, cleaning one with another. I'll need to show him how to behave in the courtroom. The longer he sits, the more he fidgets, and the more he tries to stop. His movements seem contrived and awkward, and he slouches more and more the longer the silence goes on.

Slouching is common, but some clients will squirm, some will start talking, keep talking until we stop them. A few take this experiment in stride except for the impossibility of a natural place for their hands. It sounds cruel, but quickly tells us much about a client. In fact, I enjoy this part of the size-up, especially now that the image of the clock in my father's house is gone. I feel good about my read here, and a mild, intoxicating sense of pride, maybe even self-worth, rises like the light scent of a passing woman who turns back to glance at me.

As for Mrs. Armstor, she'll likely be a problem herself, but not for the same reasons. My guess is that Meghan Armstor isn't yet thirty, and that makes her at least fifteen, maybe twenty years younger than her husband. She's dressed "to the nines," as my father would have said. At first glance, what stands out most is her beauty. Her skin is tanned, deep and even from regular salon sessions. She's taken it a shade too far, and red-tinged freckles emerge around the gold locket on her chest above the V-neck of her white sweater, the foreshadowing of age spots in years to come. Her breasts seem larger than they are... if that makes any sense. Thick blonde hair cascades around her shoulders but seems always in place. Her makeup is flawless, and her nails are a red so deep that it makes me want to lean backward and peer under the conference table to see if I'm right about open-toed sandals and matching toenails.

But things aren't always as they seem, and the longer I study her, the lean shapeliness of her body takes on a sharp edge. Her nose seems to grow more pointed. Her makeup hides budding crow's feet in the corners of her eyes, but not entirely, and the edges of her mouth are angry with their own creases.

She's severe. That will never do. After several days in court, the jury will see it too and lose any connection they had with either of them. I often wonder where all the women like Shirley—

my wife—went. She and Margaret, my secretary, oh, they're different women, but each with a selfless quality that a man can trust, even fall in love with. I've seen countless Mrs. Armstors throughout the years and wonder what spell they cast beyond the universal good looks that accompany them so that husbands never catch on to that in-it-for-herself element that ultimately leads to the inevitable divorce and the Solomon-like divisions of house, car, kids, and money.

I can almost see the diminutive Armstor fidgeting like a nervous mouse and his wife beside him like a stone, catatonic from some unknown and unvented anger but with a homicidal danger rising from her like heat from a vent.

Margaret will have to spend some time with her. By the time the trial begins, she'll have Meghan looking just as prim and neat as Margaret herself *and* with a fresh-faced innocence to go with her youth: a sincere young woman beside her man who stands falsely accused.

"So, what's this about the mortgage on my house?" Armstor asks.

"Well, it's necessary, Sam, and it's for your own protection," I say. "With our firm holding a mortgage and note on the house for its full value, anything the feds do after that will be junior to our lien. We'll be able to protect your home."

"But then you'll have the equity tied up. How will I know you'll give it back?"

He doesn't look the part, but Armstor's tough, unwilling simply to take mankind at its word. It probably surprised the executives at RoneCraft as much as it does me.

"I understand your concern, Sam. But we're on your side here. We represent you."

"How much is this going to cost—altogether, I mean?"

I glance at Jerry and wait for him to respond. He sits in his contrived pose, fingertips touching. The bastard isn't going to say anything.

"Look, Sam," I say, "there's no way to be sure. But I can tell you we've seen this cost as little as half a million and as much as five to defend by the time we're all done, that is."

Armstor leans back in his chair and looks at his wife. She looks down for a moment and nods. Armstor leans forward again. "All right. You can have the mortgage. Is that enough?"

My own mouth opens involuntarily, but Jerry speaks first. "What other assets are there?" He smiles. The signature smile again warms to put Armstor at ease. But he looks right through Jerry. It's amusing that this little man has my too-slick partner figured out.

Jerry's nostrils flare as he bores in. "We need to know, Samuel. Understand, the Feds will likely appeal our mortgage position and try to claw back the lien to insert their own. But that's not so easy, and our lien affords some protection for you."

Armstor looks at his wife, who nods again. "Well, we've got just over sixty million dollars."

Ellen leans back in her chair. Jerry doesn't move except for relaxing the pressure on the tips of his fingers and flashing a glance at me. I've been blind-sided as if, in chess, I'd left my queen unprotected.

Armstor speaks again. "It's part of the bonuses I've received over the past several years. I took my stock options each year, and as the value went up, I exercised them as soon as they vested and, of course, if they were in the money far enough. So now we have sixty million in cash. It's all offshore, and I haven't paid taxes on any of it."

Jerry puts his hand on Armstor's sleeve as the gel in his hair takes on a sinister sheen. "Samuel, this is serious business we're about to undertake. The money you deposit with us will be safe in our trust account. We, of course, are going to use it in your defense. But the fact is, defending you will cost a great deal of money. You may even be financially stressed by the end of this. But you'll be a free man, and we'll be able to help you regain your life."

"We've won many such cases, Sam," I add. "Even the two

we didn't win, the client went on probation, never spent a minute in jail."

Jerry nods in agreement, then smiles more than he should, which tells me I've gone too far and should say no more. But I try to repair the damage. "You're in good hands here, is all I'm saying, Sam." I start to fidget myself now as Jerry's smile evaporates any sense of self-worth I've accumulated.

"Winston is right, of course, Samuel. But we need to recognize the tough new laws for corporate malfeasance that have been passed. Instead of a thousand-dollar fine for financial misstatement, there's no limit. It's based on the crime itself, and the judge has wide discretion. Instead of two years in prison, it's twenty." Jerry stops and lets his words soak in. Armstor's fidgeting increases until he's almost shaking. "Now, we're not going to let that happen, Samuel, but we need to have the resources available." He puts his other hand on Armstor's forearm. "This is a bad situation, Samuel. We can make it turn out right."

Armstor flushes and the red in his cheeks rises like a wave to his wrinkled brow, where it stops, making the top of his head seem paler than it is. He looks at his wife, but she's turned to granite. She didn't move when Jerry spoke except to deepen the hardened corners of her mouth.

Samuel Armstor wipes one hand over his eyes and back across his head. He sits up and looks at me, an angry little boy. "Well, okay, I'll authorize a wire transfer of ten million. But I want an accounting, goddamn it, every month." Armstor still has some fight in him. He'd worked hard to get that money, regardless of how it came, and wasn't going to give it up easily. Still, the money means he's scared.

"Good," Jerry says and nods to Ellen. "Jennifer has the papers." Ellen leaves the room to get the wire transfer authorization. Armstor pulls his wallet out of his jacket and sorts through a set of cards. The sexless fingers work the small pieces of paper as if it's a disgusting act. By the time he finds the account number, Ellen is back. Armstor signs it along with the mortgage papers.

Jerry touches Armstor's sleeve again. Now, the shiny hair is joined by a shiny forehead made greasy from a day at our trade. "Uh, we need you to sign our engagement letter. It authorizes us to represent you." Jerry slides another set of documents toward the client. "We're on point now, Samuel." Jerry's arm sweeps across Ellen and me. "You and Mrs. Armstor should go home. We've got work to do, and we'll get back to you in the next two weeks."

Samuel Armstor's hands remain in his lap. "What should I do?"

"Go home, relax," Jerry repeats. "It'll be important to take care of yourself now. You're going to be under a great deal of pressure, and the two of you need to take it easy for a few days." Mrs. Armstor picks up a pen and signs the documents, then stands up to leave.

"Meghan," Jerry says, "when we get to court, we'll need you there." She nods. Jerry glances at me, but he doesn't need to; I'm on task now. I stand and take Meghan Armstor by the elbow. It tenses as if she doesn't like being touched.

"I'll take you out to meet my assistant. Her name is Margaret. She'll spend a few minutes with you and talk about the trial, what to expect—even though we're months away from a court date." Her lips purse. "Just come with me," I say.

When I return to the conference room, Armstor is reading the engagement letter. He objects to the firm having the right to settle the case. Jerry smiles. "The money you've entrusted to us will make certain you have full control of any settlement." He crosses out that provision and initials beside it. Armstor points to the clause where the firm reserves the right to represent them in any future book or movie.

"Samuel." Jerry's face is serious, in full counselor mode. "Our firm has several specialties. One of them is that we know how to restore our clients' wealth. This may come to nothing.

In fact, it probably will come to nothing. But if you do get the opportunity to rebuild your life from the ashes of the ordeal you're about to go through, you'll want us representing you."

Armstor relents. He spends another ten minutes with the contract but only pretends to consider each paragraph. In the end, he's a beaten man, at least for this battle, if not the war, and concedes everything else. In my father's prime, this point in the client relationship would have been referred to as "seizing his balls." It's still an appropriate metaphor, although Jerry has no taste for vulgarity while I, yes, I am only the titular head of the firm anyway, so what right do I have to set the tone?

Margaret ushers Mrs. Armstor into the room faster than Meghan is used to moving. It annoys her. Her husband looks up at her, then back at Jerry. "Okay," he said, "I'll sign this—but with a full accounting, a *full* accounting."

Jerry nods. "Of course."

Armstor signs the contract as Ellen returns. She leans over the table and signs as notary. The fact she's so much larger than him is amusing. She's about his height but has gained weight in the last year. Still attractive, just bigger. I once mistook her interest in me as more than just kissing up to the boss. She'd been with the firm for two years as a junior staff attorney when Jerry tapped her to specialize in corporate malfeasance cases. She isn't particularly bright, but she does keep up on accounting rules and can work like a dog. But she's high maintenance, always in need of an ear, and it fell to me to be that ear. We'd go to the bar at the Broadmore twice, maybe three times a week.

Ellen needed to be touched. She was always putting her hand on my arm, rubbing forearm to forearm at the bar, reaching around me and pretending to take lint off the back of my suit while her puffy, powdery cheek came within an inch of my own, its lilac talc tempting a sneeze. She'd talk about work, about growing up in southern Ohio, her family, her cat, the men she'd dated and how hard it was to find a good man. I wasn't especially attracted, but her talk of men seemed like an invitation. One night, I interrupted as she was complaining about how her body retained water and asked if she wanted to go upstairs to the room the firm kept at the hotel. She turned to me with eyes full of something more than surprise.

"Winston, you...well, you're, I mean, you're attractive and all that, but..." It was the "all that" that bothered me most. I got myself out of there, albeit in a clumsy manner, by just getting up and leaving. For months, Ellen could hardly look at me. I finally told her I was sorry for what happened, that she didn't need to avoid me and that we'd just go on as we had before the incident at the Broadmore. She liked the idea, but took it several more months before I could no longer detect her aversion to me as the fallen father figure.

Meghan Armstor leans in beside Ellen. Her dark fingers next to Ellen's puffy, pale hands make them look sickly. Ellen does retain water, and it makes her whole body puffy. But there's something in the fleshy, pale, anxious woman, poured into tight but stylish dresses, that screams of a passion barely held at bay. In her prime, Shirley, who looks nothing like Ellen, could emit that same intense sexuality when she wanted to. That was one of her magic tricks, the ability to take me down with a look, a way of walking, a certain hesitation of her hand held in front of her while I waited to see what it meant—if it meant anything, which it often did, and often did not. Shirley was the queen of intermittent reinforcement. At the same time, I could trust her. I could trust her when she had me in that hypnotic state. It was... it was... it was love, I guess. I look away.

Ellen whisks the documents off the table, telling Armstor she'll mail him a copy. Jerry stands up, shakes hands, smiles warmly, and leaves. I'm just as startled as my clients at being so quickly abandoned. Then the room has an empty feeling, lonely almost, because something residual lingers like an odor, but not an odor.

But I rise to the occasion. "Let me see you to the elevator, Sam, Mrs. Armstor."

"Call me Meghan," she says. She reaches out to shake my hand, and the touch of hers is both soft and strong and tells me she actually likes to be touched, but only on her terms. "We might as well drop the formality." Her voice remains flat, lacking all emotion, but her eyes examine me with interest, I think.

I open the door, and we make our way down the hallway. Margaret looks up as we pass her desk. I can feel her eyes. For years, Margaret was just there, just my secretary. But since Shirley's cancer returned, she seems always to be watching as if gathering information, sometimes looking through me, taking me apart as if I were some machine in need of repair. I'm certain she knows the worst about me and doesn't like it. At the same time, an affirmation passes from her, something like respect. I could spend a thousand years trying to figure out why she stays with me. Most of the time, I tell myself that once Dad is dead, she'll leave the firm. On a good day, I pretend she really does like me.

I stop in front of the elevator with the Armstors. The clock overhead says five thirty-three. I'll be ten, maybe fifteen minutes late to meet Paula. When the doors open, I can feel myself shooing the couple in and hope they don't notice, but Meghan's face has the same dissatisfaction as when Margaret hurried her. Her eyes pass across mine in a hard glance.

Armstor holds the door, steps partway out of the elevator and whispers, "I need to talk with you alone. I'll call you."

It takes me a second to register what he said. I blink, stalling until I can calculate the timing. "Call me tomorrow morning," I say, "at eleven. I'll be here." Armstor steps back and nods as the doors close. I stare at the metal seam in the elevator's wood panels and wonder if I should mention this to Jerry.

Chapter 3

I watch as Paula swings her legs out of bed, sits up and stares at herself in the dressing table mirror. She often examines herself closely, and I enjoy watching.

She is short, the first thing most people notice. She claims to be five feet tall, but if so, it's the product of liberal rounding. Her face is narrow, has an upturned nose that's attractive when she doesn't wear those clunky, black-rimmed glasses. She keeps her hair in the short, page boy style that, with a few head wags, shakes into place after a shower. She's a runner and has the lean, almost anorexic body of a Kenyan marathoner. Her legs, though, are of European stock with muscled calves almost as large as her narrow thighs, capable of carrying twice her weight. But she has delicate ankles that I like to kiss. I watch as she cups her hands under her breasts. It looks aggressive and sexy, but the truth is, she's tentative in bed. It often leaves me doubting myself.

She doesn't know how intently I study her. The more I do, the more conscious I am of my own body and the higher I pull the covers over my soft stomach, over the thickened breasts of a man's middle age. I'm a victim of excess. No, not obese, but I'm, should I say, *full* when I'm naked. I eat when it's time, or when I'm with someone, or just to eat. I drink far too much, usually beyond the five o'clock cocktail hour. Unlike Jerry, I can skip it altogether, and even more unlike Jerry, I seldom stop at one dry martini as he does. I wish Paula would shower so I didn't have to get up in full view of her and pass by in my sloppy self.

"You going to take a shower?"

"No," she answers, "at least not yet."

I look at the clock and start to get up when she changes her mind. In a few minutes, the sound of water muffles through the bathroom door.

For most of Paula's life, she wanted to be taller. I tried to convince her that height was overrated, and I think she finally came to believe me. Paula was double parked in front of the office one day when she saw Shirley enter the building. Cancer had stooped Shirley's nearly six-foot frame. Her large but elegant bearing was lost in pathetic, hunched shoulders that hid the cavities where her sagging breasts once were. She'd been stooped by cancer, by life, and maybe her three decades with me. That night, Paula confronted me with what she called our "wrongful love." Seeing Shirley had moved her to pity, to the point she suggested we stop seeing each other. I protested.

Paula is exactly half my age, and spending time with her is like being alive again. I admit the cliché, but it's not just her youth. There's no rack of pills, no stack of decorating magazines next to every cushioned armchair in the house. There's no dry, pointless cough, no stale scent of illness, none of the overwhelming signs of life coming to an early end. Some days, there's nothing at all of Shirley, and that absence has a finality to it on the one hand and yet something like a reprieve for me. I don't understand it.

As I said, Paula's a runner. She has an energy level I've never had. Even when she sleeps, it's a tight sleep where her body moves as one, not in the disjointed, centipede-like segments that Shirley rolls in different directions, especially when she's in pain.

In the end, Paula got over her guilt, or so it seems, while mine still pursues me daily. I half suspect it was more her tenuous job situation than her love for me, even though she professed it. I first met her a few years ago when she worked for an advertising agency. She was just out of college. Just after

Dad retired, I decided to modernize, start marketing the firm and hired her company to create an image-building campaign.

I made an impression on her from the beginning, cutting my best imposing frame, The Wrinkled Forehead, The Thoughtfully Raised Eyebrow, The Whole I'm-In-Charge-Here Look. I can be threatening, or at least once upon a time I was, and she took me as the genuine article. She came up with the idea of putting me in television commercials. "We'll capitalize on your 'take charge' manner, Mr. Williamsen," she'd said. I thought it bold of her, if a bit naïve. After shooting commercials an entire day, she changed her mind and thought we ought to go with print media instead. Eventually, Jerry killed the whole campaign. He believed advertising was nothing more than "open pandering to a baser form of humanity" and that we'd have every "down-and-outer in here with I-done-been-wronged-lawsuits of every ilk." Coming from Jerry, the country music tone in his description sounded more common and insulting than humorous. Then he raised my father's mantle and said we couldn't base the future of the firm on contingency fees. I never found out why Paula thought the commercials wouldn't work, but I suspect that when seen through the lens of the camera, my façade is penetrated, and the man I really am is exposed like an x-rayed tumor in the lung.

Sometime later, maybe a year, I ran into her in the bar at the Broadmore. She was there with a few of her co-workers who were taking her out on her last day at work. When the economy slipped, she was laid off from the ad agency.

In most respects, Paula's a sensible woman. But that night, she must have decided to let go and do the unexpected. I was sitting in a corner of the bar, caught her eye and waved until she felt compelled to come by my table. Her friends soon abandoned her, and before the night was over, she'd told me her whole life's story, how she and her father "had issues," how she suffered when her mother died, how she was planning to go back to school and get a Master's degree in Fine Arts, that she painted and liked the subtly of watercolors.

I told her I'd have become a writer except for that visit from my father in my sophomore year of college, the one he replayed in the foyer of the office. It *had* put me back on track to law school. Still, I majored in literature and surprised myself with what I could resurrect from those college days. We talked about Dylan Thomas' lyricism and W.B. Yeats' obsession with Byzantium, arguing it was an artistic symbol in opposition to the terse physical world we endure daily. I waxed eloquently on the lost generation, the Left Bank nineteen-twenties group: Hemingway, Samuel Beckett, F. Scott Fitzgerald. Then on to the Beatniks: Allen Ginsberg with *Howl* and Jack Kerouac, about whom I spoke as if I'd sat in the back seat of the huge Hudson listening to Sal and Dean as they careened across the country in *On the Road*.

We drank a lot and, by one in the morning, were in room 1733 mauling each other. We shared aspirin and a shower in the morning, downloaded Yeats' *Sailing to Byzantium* from the internet and made love again before noon. We've, as they say, been a couple ever since.

Cynical as I am, I suspect love and unemployment were intermingled at our inception. But her current job at Nordstrom notwithstanding, she's still with me. I'm content to ignore the practicalities that hold her. And we haven't talked about art or literature since that night.

The water in the shower stops. In a moment, she is standing at the foot of the bed with a towel wrapped around her. Even sideways, it covers her breasts and reaches below her knees. Self-conscious or not, I go to her and try to cup her breasts in my hands from behind. She pulls away. "You going to shower?" she asks.

"It's getting late, maybe a quick one, but then I've got to go." I slip into the bathroom and out again in five minutes. Paula is back in bed. "You're not leaving?" I ask.

"No, not yet. I want to stay, maybe leave in the morning. Is that okay?"

"Sure. Stay as long as you want. But you've got to leave in the morning. We've got a client coming in tomorrow," I lie, "and we're putting him up here." Something about this bothers me. She has never stayed before, and I wonder at her motives.

I also don't like the fact that she watches as I pull my tee shirt over my head. I know I look better with the flabby flesh that hangs over my belt partially hidden by the shirt. By the time I get my suit back on, I feel younger. The jackets of each of my suits have padded shoulders, an extra measure my tailor, Jerome, adds to help me cut an athletic figure regardless of the truth. That image passes away in layers as I undress. Now I stand in front of the mirror where the grey hair brings me back, just past middle age, and I feel like I have more time left. It's almost hopeful.

"Next Friday, we'll have something special brought in for dinner," I say. She smiles and waves as I leave.

I reach over and touch Shirley's shoulder as I ease myself into bed. I'm careful not to reach around too far. Shirley has had a radical double mastectomy. After nine months of chemotherapy and radiation, the cancer was back in less than sixty days. I've never seen the scars from her surgery, and that was a year ago. She insists on wearing a protective bra and refuses to let me see what she looks like. I've tried to care, but she won't let me get close, not to her body, not to her.

Now she's on a seven-days-on-fourteen-days-off chemo regimen that seems worse than the disease. She's begun talking about stopping the treatments since the doctors tell us they can't cure her... something about a more aggressive type of cancer. Chemo makes her so ill she can barely talk to me, much less pretend we've any type of relationship. The off-weeks could be better between us, but I don't try anymore. Besides, her sister Carol is with her nearly all the time during the day, and I can hardly tolerate the woman.

Still, I always touch Shirley's shoulder when I get into bed. It's the one thing I do that tells her I care about her. And I do care. Sometimes, she puts her hand on top of mine, and I feel the same touch, the one she's had for thirty years—the slow sliding back and forth of cool fingers across my hand, up along my wrist. It would be nothing. But it's not nothing. At times, that touch penetrates my core and finds a place inside me I've forgotten was there at all.

I cry sometimes, but never so she'd know it; at least she's never acknowledged it. At times, it tickles until I can hardly stand it, but I really don't want her to stop. In fact, I crave it.

Shirley groans and says something that I can't hear. "I didn't mean to wake you," I say. "Please, go back to sleep."

She rolls over on her back. "I said, 'Did you get everything done that you needed to?' With your client?"

"For now, yes. But we're getting together in the morning again at the office."

"Uh-huh." She seems to doze until she says, "Is he staying at the Broadmore?"

"No, he isn't. He lives here, in Chicago."

"Oh, Margaret thought you were at the Broadmore."

"I was," I admit. "We had dinner there, then met in the bar," I lie.

"Did you see Jeffrey?"

Jeffrey is the late-shift bartender at the hotel. He wears the nicest white shirts, a stiff starch and a flawless black tie. Few know he has on shorts and low-top Keds beneath the white apron. It's an odd sight to all but the regulars when he steps out from behind the bar and tells us how his son, Steve, is holding his own with some sweaty Florida triple-A baseball team. But more recently, I'd see the boy greeting and seating patrons in the bar, his head shaven, the triangular fractional goatee just beneath his lower lip—his soul patch—dyed a bright red. Taken together, they remind me how we are all something less than our façade.

"Yes, I saw Steve, too." I make a point of noting who's in the bar and making sure they see me. Jeffrey's value as an alibi for the regulars assures a certain level of business and tips that easily exceed his wages. I worry that he hasn't trained Steve in this art.

"Isn't he playing baseball?"

"Guess not."

I want to ask how her appointment went, but I don't. I don't have the energy to go there since what she is going through is so much more than my own feeble haunts. I can see the logic of it. But I'm not able to feel it, and that very knowledge just adds another brick in my gut. Still, Shirley seems satisfied without closure to our conversations. They just end, like an unfinished bridge, jutting into the air halfway across a gorge. The hollow, fearful feeling I'd battled earlier today lurks, waiting for its opening. I try to rush to sleep before it gains a foothold I can't shake loose. In the end, it's futile.

I ease slowly out of bed, out of the room and downstairs, where I turn on every light in the den. I pull the rubber band off an unread *Wall Street Journal,* but that doesn't work either, and the panic I feel at sinking slowly into the soup of desolation calls for strong measures. I seize Shirley's picture from my desk. It offers up only guilt. But guilt, when intensely focused on its source, is better than the invisible shifting butterfly my mind and body become when facing myself alone.

The picture was taken a few months before the first discovery of cancer, at the end of August nearly four years ago. She was tan and firm and lean from a summer on the tennis court. With her size and reach, Shirley hit an imposing, if not always accurate, ball. It was hard and fast enough to make most of the friends we played with dread facing her. I was proud of her, proud to be seen with her, proud to play tennis with her, as trite as that sounds.

I notice for the first time that, in this picture, her eyes

have hope in them, something I haven't seen for a long time. After many years of my philandering, there wasn't much fight left in them, but hope persisted. Today, even that's gone, cut out with her breasts.

"Can't sleep?" I look up to see Shirley standing, or rather, leaning in the doorway. She has on the robe I've come to hate since she sometimes wears it all day long. Her brown wig is out of place, but no more than usual. Carol keeps it clean and rotates it with one exactly like it each week. I can see her nails are red and neat, another one of Carol's simian-like habits. I should be grateful, but I'm not just because it's Carol, and I don't like Carol.

"No, guess I should have spent some time unwinding first." Shirley takes the armchair on the side of my desk. I lean back to show her how relaxed I am.

"I remember when you'd come home after a big trial. Well, after you'd been at the bar with your friends after a big trial. It didn't matter how much you'd had to drink; you still couldn't sleep unless you spent some time in here." She looks around the den, up at the built-in bookshelves above the credenza behind me.

I smile. "I remember," I say. "It didn't matter if we'd won or lost."

We fall silent as if we'd uncovered some failing of mine. It was true, though. During the years I spent in litigation, I'd celebrate, regardless of winning or losing, since the thing to celebrate was that the case was over. I've already said I worked hard to defend my clients. But decades of defending what one doesn't believe in has destroyed the bravest warrior. You can only imagine what it does to a lesser man.

I look up at Shirley and realize why she's up this time of night. The first of the seven-day run of chemo has the opposite effect from the other days. She has more strength, is more alert, and has an appetite. All that goodness is given back the very next morning, and she's further drained day by day until there seems to be less of her left than before the treatment, a net loss. By the end of the week, she's assumed the grey cast of her dingy housecoat; "my oldest friend," she calls it.

I met Shirley in law school. She discovered she really wasn't interested in the law, something I could relate to. Instead, she went back to college to become a teacher, which she never did either.

She came from a blue-collar life and was the first on either side of her family to go to college. Her father worked in a chemical plant along the sour, smoke-belching coast of Lake Michigan, where dozens of industrial sites sprawl from Chicago toward Gary, Indiana. Every time I drive on the I-90 Skyway, the twisting industrial steam rising into the sky reminds me of where Shirley grew up, a two-bedroom bungalow with rotting window sills. The house was perennially in need of paint.

Her father was a quiet, almost sullen man who grew coarse and angry when he drank and then talked too much about his tour in Korea. He died of a heart attack at sixty-seven.

Her mother was even quieter on the outside, but she'd put the notion in her daughter's head that education was the way out of their hand-to-mouth existence. For a while, I envied Shirley, having a mother so capable of protecting her from her father when he was drunk, and he changed so incredibly from his quiet, simple, decent demeanor.

Her sister Carol escaped through marriage to a bright but not particularly ambitious man with the intelligent-sounding name of Randolph Webster. He's an adjunct history professor plying his itinerant trade at several small colleges.

No one had heard from either of her two brothers since their mother died of cancer nearly fifteen years ago, and Shirley would admit to being helpless when it came to them. She said they were clones of their father—"working men and lost most of the time."

Carol grew very close after Shirley first became ill, and their relationship continues to tighten even as cancer pulls her toward death. Carol long ago found God, or, rather, Jesus, and she's out to save Shirley before it's too late and she passes on to eternal damnation.

I've always had the deepest fear of the deeply religious. They generally aren't any better than the rest of us, which makes them seem worse for professing a belief they don't live up to. I've learned all this the hard way. Despite my cynicism, I tend to trust everyone until they give me a reason not to, and they usually do, especially those proclaiming the love of Jesus.

I should know by now the fixed nature of humankind. Of course, all I need to do is look in the mirror. But my sins are of weakness, of flesh, of temptation given into as I search for a way out of reality by draining what intellect I have into baser passions. These are not passions of greed but of panic. And that makes me different from those who profess the heart of Christ but whose goal is to crush and build an empire on the dust of the bones of others. Or, as Blake put it, "drive your plow over the bones of the dead."

I've concluded that the Christian doctrine of salvation through grace has let them off the hook—unable to earn heaven, one gets unending forgiveness through faith alone. If God can make a mistake, it is probably this: that toxic combination we mortals manipulate of freewheeling free will coupled with unlimited grace and forgiveness. So why the hell live to a higher standard in the first place? None of this insight, I realize, makes me superior.

So, what *are* the consequences I inflict? I didn't give Shirley her cancer. Well, not the cancer that slowly eats her with each heartbeat. Mine is a form of emotional cancer, yes, but is that as cruel as what her own mother gave her: oncological predestination? I haven't meant to harm her, but neither have I stopped the harm and so I've compounded it. But here, I need to pause since I sense the problem, see, is that I play both man and God—commit what mayhem I will then forgive myself for it. Okay, I've gone far enough down that rabbit hole.

I like to think my inability to support her has made her

self-reliant and strong enough to get through this inevitable journey. And this is another reason to hate Carol: she gives Shirley hope where I have none.

"Well, I'm going to bed," she says. "Goodnight." I watch as she pushes herself upright with arms, legs, the chair, anything she can find to help. By the time I realize I should help her, she's standing.

"Wait," I say. I don't know how long we've sat in silence, but only now feel how awkward it is.

She sits down again, a process nearly as painful to watch as getting up. "Yes?" she asks.

"We just, well, we haven't spent much time like this recently," I say. "I mean, if you're tired, we can..."

"No," she says almost too loudly for the distance between us. "I'm fine. Of course, I'm not looking forward to how I'll feel tomorrow, but I'm good now."

"Good," I say. But now I have a problem because I need to say something more, and I've run on empty so long that our conversations end before time expires. "How's Carol?" I ask.

Shirley smiles. "She's better than I am, Winston." Chuckles. "I know that's probably bad news as far as you're concerned. The two of you should try to get along, you know."

"We get along," I lie.

"If that's the case, then so do the Palestinians and Israelis. Actually, though, if you gave it a chance, you might find you've more in common than you think. In fact, and I don't want to depress you, but the two of you are quite alike."

I smile to cover my fear that Shirley knows of my internal demons. I study her face to see if what she said was a reference to her sister or if there's something more. "Ho!" I say. "Time for me to climb to the roof and jump."

She laughs. "I thought so. Try not to scream on the way down. You'll wake the neighbors."

"I'll remember that. Maybe I should take Carol up there with me, see who reaches the ground first." It went too far.

Shirley forces a smile, but it's a false image.

She sighs. "I know I said I wasn't tired, but maybe I was too optimistic."

"Can't have that," I try again, "being too optimistic." It isn't funny, and the life in her face drains as I watch. I wonder at my stupidity and wish I could take back what I'd said. But then, I'm not even sure that I caused the leak in her fragile spirit. Life itself drains through the thin walls of her soul; a new break opens each time an old one scabs over. She struggles to her feet again, and I just watch again.

"Goodnight," she says.

"Hope you sleep well," I respond to her back as she leaves.

Silence surrounds me until I feel the haunting emptiness begging my depression to fill it up. I summon anger to ward it off.

While Shirley and I find ourselves alone more than I like, we're usually alone by ourselves, seldom in the right place at the right time to be alone together. It was a good spot we were just at, but we—I mean I—squandered it. I know I push her away, unable to tolerate the naked feeling of a moment too near, too close, and to tell her I will miss her sitting there. Right there in the front of my mouth, yet never spoken. I get up, move to the chair she vacated, and sit down in the pale warmth that remains. She surrounds me. She's not here, not really, and still, she lingers where she'd sat, the warmth of her frail body, the scent of illness hovering over the remnants of perfume that Carol dabs behind her ears each morning.

I wonder if this is what it will be like once she's gone, that some sign she was once here will linger. Or will there be nothing left but her magazines? I seldom let myself get this far: *Nonsense.*

After leaving law school, Shirley struggled with her decision and what it said about her. She was supposed to set an example for other women—"rise above the anonymity of the weaker sex and the underclass," she'd once said to a friend, to take her place beside men of power and stature. I suspected it terrified her to think of stretching herself.

She finally said she didn't want equality; she wanted me. We were married in my final year, and she worked part-time while I finished law school with my father's financial support.

She owned up to her fear of failing on our honeymoon. She told me she felt like a trapeze artist, afraid to let go and trust that another trapeze would be there. I remember feeling angry, thinking that she was too much like my mother. But it was too late. We were married, and I'd have to make the best of it. Foolish, or worse, that's what I felt at the time.

Dad didn't like the fact that his only son married into a working-class family. But Mother found Shirley "more charming than most of the snobs we know and much better than the women Winston chases on his own." Dad relented. It may have been because of Mother's influence, but I couldn't believe it at the time. It was more likely he became distracted and just forgot about the relationship until we announced we were getting married.

Shirley wanted to be a mother but couldn't have children. She wanted to adopt, but I wouldn't agree to it, and now, late at night, beside her, as she tries to rest from the day-long struggle against cancer, I'm certain it was the right decision. I believed then, and I know now I have little to offer as a father.

Even with our problems, I can't believe our life together has always been bad—at least not until Shirley became ill. We live in a gated community, in a home that Shirley dotes over, always redecorating some part of it, so much so that we've redone everything, everywhere, and more than once. We had a blessed existence: we traveled a lot and patronized the arts. We have investments and position and power. Well, that's what I tell myself. But the very thought lifts the haunting, hollow, meaningless feeling back into consciousness.

Shirley carried herself well for so many years. Besides being tall and thin, she had deep-set eyes beneath dark bangs. Her lines bore long dinner party dresses with an easy elegance. But sometimes, her simple background would show through in a plain comment or when she didn't understand something, like the client from Charleston who talked about his daughter's coming-out party. Shirley was curious and, I thought, far too prying in trying to understand the nature of a coming out, which, she admitted to a large group during dinner, seemed so distant from her own upbringing.

Friends had to forgive her lack of social sophistication, and it embarrassed me. But they always did forgive her. Who wouldn't forgive Shirley? Sweet Shirley Williamsen, sweet, kind, caring Shirley Williamsen.

Chapter 4

The tapping starts quietly. I know it's there, but don't jolt from my stupor until it sounds like a hammer on an iron tube. Then it stops. It brings me around long enough to catch a glimpse of Shirley's picture on my desk, so I must be at home, in my den. But the clock next to it is just like the one at the office. It reads eleven-thirteen, and the date says Saturday, May 4. Piece by piece, I remember I'd slept on the leather settee in my den, got up early and came into the office, where I'd done nothing but doze for what now looks to be three hours.

And the tennis picture of Shirley... here it is.

The tapping starts again, faint at first, then louder and louder until I realize it's coming through my open door from down the hall. I stand and limp from my office on knees that have stiffened. They remind me how my body takes longer each morning to limber up.

By the time I round the corner, I'm moving better and see Samuel Armstor standing on the other side of the plate glass entrance to the office suite. He's tapping his keys on the inch-thick glass just above the monogrammed letters: *Williamsen and Williamsen, Attorneys at Law.*

Armstor looks smaller than I remember from yesterday. He wears a white shirt and light grey slacks that wash the color from his face. Without a tie and jacket, he seems like an unfinished cartoon character, an anorexic Wimpy from the Popeye cartoons of my childhood.

I step back as I open the door to let him in and notice the navy-blue jogging suit I had put on to sleep in last night. I slowly put the final pieces together. I couldn't face sleeping next to Shirley. Our short conversation was just too nearly intimate, and I opted for the den but really hadn't slept well there. I splashed water on my face and combed my hair, then came to the office knowing Armstor would be stopping in but, for some reason, was unable to take in the fact that I wasn't dressed for a client visit.

It's not vanity. Without my suit, I'm fairly certain the last vestiges of lawyerly façade are gone, and I might as well be naked. Jerry won't like it if I somehow blow this deal today.

"Sam, I'm surprised to see you. I was waiting for your call." I'm always surprised by the normal tone in my voice when nothing seems normal, and I wonder where this level of control comes from since I'm certain it's not from inside me.

"Well, this is too important, and I had to see you in person." I lock the glass doors while Armstor disappears around the corner. I barely catch up to him as he sits down by my desk. He looks around.

"There's no one else here, Sam." Armstor still says nothing, and I speak to avoid the silence. "Well, things were different when my father was in charge. Nowadays, no one works on Saturday." We just look at each other. "What can I... what's this about? We haven't got much to tell you about the case since you were just here yesterday."

Armstor slides down in his chair. He straightens his legs out and sags his shoulders as he shrinks to an even smaller frame. "I've got more to tell you. But I need to know if I *should* tell you."

"About the case?"

He studies his fingernails. "Not exactly. But it *will* be before long."

"I'm your lawyer, Sam. You can tell me anything."

Armstor's face contorts until he seems to sneer at me. "But I need to know if you *will* keep this to yourself."

"If it can help us in the defense..."

"Fuck the defense. I need to know if I can tell you this in confidence. That is, can I tell you something, and you'll keep it from your partners?"

I shift in my chair, then lean forward and place my hands on the desk where they feel awkward. I wonder where else I might put them and half wish Jerry was here.

I sit back again and fold my arms. "All right," I say. "Tell me what you want. It won't go any further."

Armstor shuffles his chair closer to my desk. "That sixty million I told you about? Well, there's another seventy million besides that."

I lean forward and cross both arms on the desk. We've been dancing. I shuffle, he shuffles, I shuffle again. It's like a bad Humphrey Bogart movie, and I want to think about how silly we really seem, but then I realize what he said. I wonder what it means, what's between the lines. That a client isn't completely forthcoming is nothing new. In fact, it's the norm for the guilty. But I play along. "Go on."

Armstor sighs and nods. He puts his smallish hands on the desk and folds them as if in prayer. "I didn't tell you this before because it has nothing to do with these charges. But as I said, I have another seventy million."

Armstor tells me he'd been in charge of acquisition activity since 1985. Since then, in the last ten years, RoneCraft made five acquisitions. In the first one, he'd been the project manager for Janice Steward, the Chief Financial Officer. The acquisition went well, but at the end of the project, the costs exceeded the thirty-million-dollar budget by a third, nearly ten million dollars.

Steward was mad as hell, and so were the CEO and the entire board. Armstor was afraid he'd be fired. But he was able to show Steward where her own decisions caused much of the overrun, and things settled down.

Two years later, they bought another company. Again, Armstor was named acquisition manager. This time, he set up a consulting company that existed in name only. He was the company's only stockholder and made certain it was given the contract to manage the project. Then, he hired a legitimate consulting group and subcontracted the actual due diligence, accounting, legal, regulatory, and public relations work. The contract with his faux firm was based on the total cost of acquisition, in this case, eight percent of eighty million. He'd paid the accounting subcontractors three million and kept the rest. The records all went to the CFO in summary form, and she signed off the acquisition documents, the SEC filings and the shareholder reports. At the end of the year, Geoffrey Ross, Jr., the CEO, and Steward both certified the financial statements.

Armstor clears his throat. "I did essentially the same thing in three more acquisitions, getting various amounts from each deal. I mean, in the larger scheme of things, those dollars amounted to a rounding error. Besides, I knew Steward and the CEO had other, more nefarious things going on that I was starting to figure out."

Most of what he's saying sounds incredible, and I sense the unstable air around me. "So now you believe that what you did will come to light."

"Yes. If the investigation goes back five years, that would pick up the last two acquisitions only. If they go back further, they might catch all of them."

"Sam, this is disturbing. As your attorney, I can't tell anyone, but at the same time, I can't do much for you if you're guilty, and they can prove it."

Armstor sits back in his chair. "Well, that would disappoint me, Winston. I thought I was coming to the right man, someone who'd know what to do." He pauses to fondle the desk with sweaty fingers. "I'm prepared to pay you what it takes."

The air goes out of the room, but I focus on Armstor's forehead. A shiny film has emerged on his skin. "I'm not sure how I could help."

"I think you might be able to figure that out. You just need to decide whether you'll do it or not. If you agree, then I have at least one task for you. Maybe more."

I breathe. I look around my office, and the motion clears my mind. I need to find a way out: to let Armstor down easily. But I've never been propositioned this directly in more than thirty years. Just what is the man willing to do? I should tell him to get out, that we're dropping the case. But knowing that's the right thing only makes me curious.

"So, what's the bottom line?"

"Well, the case goes on just as it is. But this other matter, somehow, we keep it out of the investigation. We beat the current charges and avoid this mess."

"And?"

His eyes can't meet mine. "Think in terms of, say, half. It'll take some money to keep this quiet. But the balance we'll split."

"Wait-wait-wait-wait here: just a minute. I can't be hearing this. What about your wife?"

"She doesn't know anything about it." He leans forward and locks on my eyes. "We'll just keep it that way."

"But..."

"Look, you see how it is. She's a beautiful woman married to an ugly, short, bald old man. She used to work in payroll at RoneCraft and knew what the executive bonuses were. She saw me gaining some power in the company and knew I was starting to make big money—at least as far as she was concerned. She also knew I was divorced and came after me. So, you see, she's that kind. Not that I put up a fight or anything. But I expect she'll divorce me at some point and then may want to test the prenup. Heh, I don't regret it; any of it. At least not yet."

The sharp edge of my haunt creeps into me. It works its way up, filling my stomach, tightening my chest, and all the while pushing an avalanche of dread before it. I realize I've been staring at Shirley's picture without knowing it. When I look up, Armstor smiles as if he already has his answer.

"I can look into some things," I hear myself say.

"Good. I'll bring you a cashier's check..."

I hold my hand up. "I haven't said I'll do anything. I only said I'd look into some things, talk to some people I know." Armstor rises, nods and walks swiftly out of the office. I know it's not the only way, but he did just illuminate one way the rich get richer.

Chapter 5

Saturday is my least favorite day. It holds such promise when the sun first rises but deteriorates when I realize I've no plan for it. I often go to the office to fill the time between waking and developing a plan. Once I've exhausted that haven, I return home by mid-afternoon anxious at the day's slippage, that it'll slip some more and eventually will be gone. But still, I form no plan.

Today is spoiled further when I pull into the driveway. The session with Armstor fades, at least for now, as I spy Carol's car sitting directly in front of where I need to go to reach the garage. She must do this on purpose. She must know I'll return, that the open door and vacant spot next to Shirley's car would mean I need to drive right through where she's parked.

I consider bulldozing her out of the way with the tow bar on my Humvee. Instead, I pull up behind her car, step out, cross the brick driveway Shirley had put in last fall and enter through the garage she'd had drywalled and painted and where cedar plank wainscoting was put in just after Christmas and through the leaded glass entry door she'd had installed last month. When I reach the kitchen, Carol looks up from the newspaper she's spread across the island that Shirley had resurfaced with granite less than a year ago, replacing the ceramic tiles she'd had installed less than two years ago. "Hello, Carol," I say.

"Hi." She looks back to the paper, peering through the

half-lens reading glasses she sometimes scolds me with.

"Where's Shirley?"

Carol pulls off her glasses and observes me for a moment. "She's sleeping, Winston. You know the new chemo starts to hit her the day after treatment."

"I know that."

She puts one temple of her glasses in her mouth and sits there, still looking at me.

"What?" I ask.

"Nothing."

"Carol, what is it?"

"I was just wondering if you actually knew she was at the next level. You do remember, don't you?"

"Of course I do. I know it knocks her for a loop."

"Do you." It wasn't a question.

"Look, Carol, I know we don't see eye to eye, but for God's sake, yes. I know that."

"Don't take the Lord's name in vain, Winston."

"It's just an expression."

"It's never *just* an expression. It's God's name."

I try to focus back on Shirley. "So, how is she?"

"Haven't you been a part of this discussion? She's suffering."

"That's not what I mean. I mean, how's she doing, really? How are her spirits today?"

"You mean about her cancer?"

It's an evil question. Carol suspects me of constant unfaithfulness. And while she's not wrong, we both seem to understand the greater disservice I do is not being there for Shirley. But I can't be there when Carol's there, and Carol's always there. "Goddamn it," I say.

"Once again, don't take the name of the Lord in vain. I'd think someone in your position would be more contrite, Winston, maybe call on God instead of cursing."

"I thought Christians taught contriteness by example."

"We do. But we also admonish those who need it when they need it."

I throw my arms up. "Okay, okay. If Shirley's asleep and you're going to stay until she wakes up, I'm leaving. After all, I just own this place." I swing my arm around the room. "I just pay for the constant replacing of everything we have here."

"Don't you get down on Shirley because she redecorates. It's about all she has left that gives her pleasure. You can afford it, after all, and it gives you the freedom to ignore her. So it's no skin off your nose."

I'm tempted to dress down the self-righteous bitch, but I leave through the door to the garage instead, slamming it behind me. I get as far as the driveway and realize I have to turn around for my keys. When I enter the house, Carol is crying. Good, I think, maybe she'll back off. I grab the keys from the island and start for the door again.

"Wait. Winston. Don't go."

The desperate air in her voice stops me, and I turn around. Her mousy, short brown hair is as out of place as it usually is. As much time as she spends grooming Shirley, she doesn't seem to have time to take care of herself. She seldom wears make-up and has none on today. The daily vigil has deepened the lines in her forehead until they've taken the edge off the beauty she once had. Her nails are short: bitten off. She doesn't chew on them constantly, but once she starts, she keeps on until every nail is close to bleeding.

Despite all this, as Shirley's illness has ravaged her body, I've come to resent how much like the Shirley of old Carol is. It's not right, and the fact that she's a mess, that she doesn't take care of herself but still seems attractive compared to Shirley, only makes things worse. As I look into her eyes, I realize she'd probably been crying earlier today before I came home. I've seen her cry lots of times, but the cast on her face seems different today, as if something inside her has broken. "What is it?" I ask.

"It's Shirley." Carol wipes her eyes with the backs of her hands. "She said she's not sure she'll agree to the next level of

47

chemo if she has to go there. She says it's not worth fighting so hard just to end up feeling so sick."

"We've both heard that before. She'll feel better in a week, and then she'll get over it."

"I don't think so," she says. "Today was different. It's not the pain. She sounds almost hopeful when she talks about it like everything's clear. Like she's come to some... some understanding with... God." She looks at me, and I half expect another tirade about my lack of faith. I can see her try to blink back a new wave of tears, but they only stream faster down both cheeks. Her leaking eyes are almost pleading. "But what about us?" she asks. "What understanding has she come to with us?"

I can hardly take in the question. It's too big. Instead, I focus on the fact she has included me as if we were on the same side. She's hurting enough that I think about putting my arm around her. But the last time I did that, she pulled away. Still, as I think about Shirley, it occurs to me that I might be the one who needs to be touched.

"We'll deal with this later, Carol." I turn away with all the resolve I can muster.

"Wait. Don't go." Carol's sobs end when the door closes behind me.

Chapter 6

It's now two weeks to the day after the Armstors' first visit when I find myself with Ellen, Jerry, and Margaret in the small windowless conference room next to my office. With no window to look out of, I've spent the last few minutes thinking about Shirley.

Just as I'd predicted, she's back in the fight. She felt good enough today, in fact, that she and Carol were going to strip the wallpaper in the guest powder room and start over. Carol's tolerance of me ebbs and flows with Shirley's mental and physical state, and she's been more civil since Shirley's improved. I could almost delude myself into thinking it's because we connected—or almost did. But I know better. Besides, she hasn't referred to that afternoon since then and would probably deny it ever took place.

But here I am, now, back in the meeting. Armstor has called several times, but I've used Margaret as a human shield to avoid talking with him. The specter of getting millions of dollars still intrigues me. It's not just the money, although I've been thinking of what my life could be with it. But why me? I've let it run too long already. I close my eyes and determine I'll need to set him straight soon.

I feel Ellen's eyes on me and was planning to take the lead, but when I open my mouth to speak, my mind is blank. Jerry finally begins.

"Here's what we know. Armstor worked as a tax accountant in various line jobs before landing at RoneCraft nearly fifteen years ago. For a half dozen years, he basically worked on the financials. Then, in '85, he was tapped as the project manager for the acquisition with Jacobson Presses. After that, they moved him to the corporate office, and he's overseen every acquisition since. That's fifteen altogether.

"He kept a tight hold on each acquisition. And that's bad news. If he'd have been more open and involved more of his staff at several decision points, we'd have witnesses. But Armstor kept things under wraps. We found a memo written by the CFO in '83 during the third acquisition. In it, she complained she wasn't being kept informed and that Armstor needed to file weekly status reports with her."

I can feel them looking at me. "Did he... file the reports?" I ask.

"No one has found any, even though Armstor says he did. The Justice Department tells me they haven't found any that requires sharing with us."

"You think they're stonewalling?" Ellen asks.

"I don't know," Jerry says. "They may fight us unless we keep a judge involved. They mean to hang this on him."

"Just what *does* Justice have?" she asks.

"I can't be sure. But I doubt they have the hard evidence they thought they'd find."

I already know they don't have a thing to go on, and I find it strange, too. I'd talked with Marge Smithson, who works at the Justice Department. She's only an office assistant but has been at Justice for over twenty-five years. That makes her almost invisible on a daily basis and privy to much of what goes on. Marge spent time volunteering with Shirley for the United Way in past years. They had a falling out when they co-chaired a committee and lost contact after that.

While she doesn't particularly like me, she'd thought a lot about Shirley and was glad for the update on her condition.

She wanted to call Shirley, and I said she'd welcome it. That was all it took. She told me she'd overheard Collier Clark, the lead prosecutor, telling his boss that they'd "get this guy," that "we just need to get to discovery, get a hold of more company files, and Samuel Armstor will be all but on his way to prison." She told me they were getting a judge's order in the next couple of days, and RoneCraft would need to produce a decade's worth of internal records. After their initial review, I called her back. She said Clark sounded brave, but he's concerned he had nothing concrete on Armstor yet. He even worried privately that they'd moved too quickly and maybe too publicly in arresting him.

I can't let myself think about it. Besides, it's pretty standard stuff as I listen to Jerry and Ellen jaw through the facts. RoneCraft paid too much for each of the companies it bought. The acquisitions resulted in a lot of goodwill, just blue sky, on the balance sheet, along with too much debt. They moved much of their liability off-balance sheet to three different partnerships along with a couple of small lines of business they intended to close down anyway. The company's statistics and financial ratios improved immediately. The only sign of the partnerships came in a footnote where they listed the investment as part of their capital.

I know the rest by heart. I clear my throat. "Then the economy went bad, the partnerships couldn't pay their own way, RoneCraft's core business went in the tank, and all hell broke loose."

"Exactly," Ellen says, turning toward me. "While the partnerships filed for bankruptcy, RoneCraft lost the capital they'd invested. RoneCraft itself had borrowed heavily, and more debt, coupled with the capital write-down, meant RoneCraft itself was insolvent."

"Now for the obvious question," I say. "Why are they trying to put all of this on our man? What about the CFO, the CEO?"

Ellen laughs. "You haven't seen the news coming across

your screen saver this morning? Both are being charged today. But they've been cooperating with someone because they didn't have to face the perp-walk. They just went home and had their lawyers stand in for them."

"Obviously, they're helping paint Armstor into a corner," Jerry says. "They have friends in government—from the international contracts they'd worked on. The goal is to maybe look stupid but not criminal."

"We'll be trying to show Armstor's recommendation on accounting was legit," Ellen adds. "We aren't in too bad a shape there." She pats a stack of research files beside her. "He did make a couple of runs at the CFO during the first acquisition. Even has a memo he'd sent. If he did try to get the accounting right and was forced to do something illegal, then *he* might just be the one who looks stupid but not guilty.

"One problem, though, is that he regularly cashed in against his options. Both the CEO and CFO held on to theirs, so with the stock price down, they're out of the money. In fact, they'd borrowed heavily to buy the stock and now owe more than it's worth. Armstor turned his into cash along the way. Then he put that cash in offshore accounts. Those actions, by themselves, were legal when they occurred, but they look ugly to Joe Lunchbox sitting on the jury."

Joe Lunchbox is what I'd call Shirley's father. She objected only sporadically because I'd push back on her until she admitted it was true. I was only being honest. Ellen and Jerry are looking at me again, but I don't care.

I think of Shirley's father and wonder if he'd have seen it that way. He wouldn't have liked it, but still, he would have understood his job was to uphold the law, as sad as that is, and he'd have done the right thing—if following laws that sanction bad behavior *is* the right thing. I suddenly felt bad about the things I'd called him and those worse I'd thought of him. I feel Jerry's furtive glance and try to appear contemplative.

Jerry and Ellen continue plotting. She's uncovered a case that

Collier Clark himself had investigated. When he was done, he stood at a news conference and told the world that there was no crime, that what the executives had done was within the law even though they walked off with more than a hundred million. The media played it as if he was in league with them, and he was called on the carpet for it. I remember that just as I remember most of the bad things that happen to lawyers. Didn't think he had it coming then. But now he's on the other side, and we'll use it against him. We will, if we have a reason. Good lawyering is all it is. I stretch both arms over my head. It feels good, and the weight pressing on me lifts slightly.

I turn to Margaret. "What about Mrs. Armstor?"

Margaret puts her pen down precisely on the notepad she's been tending. She looks around at each of us and then settles her eyes on me. "I have a luncheon with her next Thursday. I'm sorry, Mr. Williamsen, but she kept putting me off."

It's odd to see her distressed. Even when I stir her to action, it's just intense, not strained as she now appears. "Do you need any help with her?"

"No. I think she understands now."

I have no doubt that Meghan Armstor could be a challenge, even for Margaret. "Good girl," I say. "I'm sure you'll have her looking Bible study pretty in no time." Margaret flinches. She doesn't like that term. Margaret's an evangelical Christian of a better breed than Carol. But even she believes that getting women to look and act as she would look and act has the greater purpose of being good for their souls.

Margaret shifts in her seat when no one speaks. For the third time in the meeting, Jerry and Ellen are looking at me, and I wish I'd said nothing. Jerry turns toward Margaret. "Thank you, Margaret. You always make a difference."

By five-thirty, the office has cleared out. May had come in a summery fashion, and the longer days tempt the tenured staff to leave early for weekend yard work while the youngsters, as we call the dozen junior staff attorneys, bail out of the high-rise office to stop by their high-rise apartments just long enough to change, then to the parks with rollerblades and dogs with Frisbees.

Even I enjoy the trip along Lakeshore Drive past the mounded gardens where tulips are nursed, their blooming lives extended by daily trimming. I'm looking forward to it tonight, too, and I wonder if I could stop near one of the colorful mounds and take in the lake, the beauty of spring rushing into summer. But the wind is still cold and strong along Lake Michigan, where white caps drive the color of water from blue to black. And the noise—cars, rush hour traffic, the occupants—all hurtling northward, southward, escaping downtown with its pointless commerce to seize what little personal joy they can after honking and flashing the finger to distraction.

But the main reason I'd stop today would be to stall for time before going home. Shirley called and set up a dinner date at home. Margaret somehow patched her through to me, and I'm still pissed at her. She's my main defenseman whose job it is to help me avoid—that is, avoid whatever may come my way without my permission.

I would delay tonight except for the fact Shirley's already called me on it. "Don't give me that 'I need to finish something up' routine," she said, laughing. "You can go in tomorrow and spend the whole day. I just want this one night, one dinner." Her voice sounded lighter than the words she used and much lighter than their meaning. But she knows that a lawyer's most effective weapon is delay.

I'm resigned. As I leave my office, I look across the foyer and notice Jerry's light is still on. I start for his office. Shirley never seems to mind when I'm late because of Jerry. I can't tell if she likes him or if she's just grateful that he sticks with me, of his ability to make the firm successful in spite of me. It's another reason to hate him.

"Hi," I say. "Working late tonight?"

Jerry looks up from the dozen or so files stacked neatly on his desk. Only one is open at a time, a habit he's meticulous about: "Don't want to confuse the cases, Winston," he'd once said. He's surprised at seeing me, though, at this time on a Friday night and knowing what he knows about Paula.

"Just another hour. Then I'm going down to Rush Street, have a little fun," he says.

Now I'm surprised. "Thought you said you were through with that place."

He shrugs his wrist, pen in hand. "Well, I'm just having dinner by myself, and then I'll observe the dance for a while."

Jerry likes to watch as people maneuver around each other in the bars, or 'meat markets,' on Rush Street. He enjoys the spectacle of the mating dance regardless of gender, especially as the night wears on. "That's when you get to see how people really are," he'd once told me. "The drinking, the atmosphere, are catalysts that release the chemical binding of moral inhibition."

He doesn't often share his plans with me. I sit down across from him, and something hopeful rises inside me. His hair has won the battle, defeated his scented gel. Its waves lean casually to one side, making him look younger, calmer, and less uptight, and I can almost see what men so inclined could be attracted to. I watch him work.

His computer is perennially logged into legal research sites, and he moves from file to mouse, mouse to file, checking on the cases the junior attorneys have selected to support our clients. I know he takes great care of the firm, of me, by doing this, and I am often torn, again, between anger and appreciation for what he does. He's the brother I didn't have, the one I'd be jealous of and about whom I could lament that Mother liked him best. Only in my case, it was Dad.

"Lots to do yet?" I ask.

He doesn't look up. "No, just a minute."

I watch as he puts down the file he holds and clicks his mouse several times as he moves it around the pad. I know he's finally logged off when I ask, "Where are you going?"

"Well, I'm not sure, but it doesn't matter. It's a light dinner I'm after. Then, some mindless observation. Then the fitness club."

I look at my watch. "Shirley's expecting me. We're having dinner tonight at home."

Jerry reclines in his chair. "That's good, Winston. How's she holding up?"

"It's getting worse," I say, "and harder for her to stay with it."

"I suppose." I sense the tension in his body subside until it's barely perceptible.

"It's going to get interesting if I can put it that way. Shirley is so sick... and Dad." I wag my head. "I guess I'll need to do something about him soon. His days at home are numbered, even with the help I've brought in. I've been thinking about filing for guardianship."

Jerry closes his eyes and then leans forward, rubbing his hands across the slate writing surface of his desk.

"We should probably talk about that, Winston."

"I don't know what there is to talk about. You see how he is."

Jerry gets up from his desk and goes to the small two-drawer fireproof file he keeps in his office. He spins through the combination and takes out a thin file, returns to his chair, lays it down and folds his hands across it. "I need to tell you something," he says. He shakes his head.

"What's this about?" I look at the file but can't read the label.

"There's just no easy way... Just over two years ago, your father came to me and asked if I'd be willing to serve as his guardian if it ever became necessary." He pauses. "Of course, I protested," he continues. "I tried to get out of it: told him that you were the one to do that." He stops again, but by now, I'm in my wait-Jerry-out mode. Still, he looks as if he could wait forever.

"Just what did he say to that?" I finally ask.

Jerry's in 'the role' now, the one where the honest lawyer levels with the client: *You're likely to go to the electric chair when this is all done. Now, I'm going to defend you the best I can, and we'll do everything possible for the best outcome, but you need to know the worst that could happen.* "Well, it was just after Shirley was diagnosed. He said he didn't think you could handle any more, that he'd be okay with it if Shirley was going to be involved, but he didn't hold out much hope for her situation in the long run."

"How the hell could he know what would happen?"

"He didn't, of course. He said he didn't have a good feeling about it. He was trying to spare you the pressure of having to take care of him and Shirley at the same time. He was concerned about you."

"Goddamned funny way of showing it," I say.

Jerry holds up his hands. "Okay, okay, Winston. I understand how you might feel. But I won't do anything without you. I'll involve you all the way if you want me to."

"Just how far has he gone? With the guardianship?"

"All the way. I have power of attorney, too. So I can manage his affairs."

"Power of attorney? You mean you have that right now? You can sign for everything?"

"You know I'd never abuse it."

"Never, huh? What about his ownership in the firm? You can vote his shares. Hell, sell them to yourself if you see fit."

"Come on, Winston, that'd be blatantly wrong, a conflict of interest that the court wouldn't stand for."

"You saying I'll need to sue you?"

"For gosh sakes, no, I'm not saying that. I'm saying that *won't* happen, that I'd *never* do anything like that."

"So I should just trust you that you won't end up with the firm, won't replace me as managing partner?"

"That would *never* happen. You're a Williamsen, the firm's namesake, for chrissake."

"I don't know if I can believe you."

Jerry closes his eyes for a moment and then levels them at me. "Okay, here's the rest of it. Your father's estate is essentially pledged to the University of Chicago, almost all of it, everything beyond estimated taxes and settlement expenses. He's stipulated a scholarship be created with his name on it."

I think I heard what he said, but none of it makes sense. Dad went to the University's law school but hadn't been an active alumnus, at least not in my memory.

"What, or who drove him to this?"

"I don't really know. He never said why, and I didn't ask. I was uncomfortable enough agreeing to what he wanted me to do and couldn't bring myself to ask him why he was leaving you out. But not entirely, you know. The will, and I have that, too... the will gives you something... shit Winston, I'm telling you more than I should. The status of his estate is a private matter." Jerry sees me wince. "I'm acting as his attorney here." That stops us both. The lighting seems harsh, and I'm starting to feel weak, enough so that my haunt creeps into my stomach again. Jerry shrugs. "Maybe he's looking for some legacy beyond the firm. Or maybe immortality. Listen, you have your percentage of the firm. You'll be all right."

I stare at Jerry as if he were an opposing attorney who'd just sealed his case against my client. He stands up. "Look, Winston, you need to think about this some. Let it sink in. We'll talk again. In fact, let's set up an appointment in the next couple of weeks. This is the kind of thing that needs to be looked at objectively."

Jerry pauses briefly, then puts the file back, checks to see the cabinet is locked, and leaves as casually as if we'd been talking about the Cubs.

I'm numb. My father never thought much of me, I know. But this goes too far. I'm family, blood. I should be the one.

I look at my watch to focus on something else. I need to

get home. I'll be nearly twenty minutes late now, and Shirley will be disappointed, and I don't want to disappoint her, not now, for some reason, especially not now.

Chapter 7

There were good years, times when we were close, husband and wife, friends and companions. Our dinner table was a place to ease myself away from the day's troubles. Our bedroom was a haven from the world. In fact, it was the one place I could lay down the sword of the law, remove the helmet of command, and cry. Shirley held me in a way that said it was all right to empty myself of the poison trapped inside from a long day of pretending what I was not. Somehow, we both knew it must never be said aloud as if, once spoken, I couldn't find the resolve to face the next day. So I would lie in her arms and whimper while she understood why. We said nothing, but the slow slide of her fingers up and down my forearm was enough.

I try to remember when we stopped connecting at that level. A dozen years ago, maybe. It angers me. But I'm also angry with her for no longer being the woman I married. I feel cheated somehow, although, in clear moments, the logic doesn't hold.

Sometimes, I imagine she's already dead. The thought brings a miserable form of guilty relief.

Shirley looks up from her untouched plate. She's dressed for dinner, and I can almost see the woman I once knew, like a shadow, a ghostly halo surrounding the shell she's become. She isn't feeling well, isn't hungry, but pretends both as well as she can.

She sips from her water glass, sets it down and smiles at

me. "So. We haven't had dinner like this for some time."

"That's true," I say, trying to sound chipper. The fact is, we haven't had dinner like this, at least not the two of us alone, for years. At one point in our lives, Shirley spent most of her time volunteering. We had a live-in servant who did the cooking. It allowed us to meet on Friday nights at our own dining room table and act as if we were in some fine restaurant. Eventually, I protested the cost of the maid, and we let her go. Shirley didn't object, but she began to cut back on volunteering, spent more time at home and started to notice things she thought needed changing. For the past several years, she's been decorating and redecorating the house. The pace at which things are done has picked up since cancer entered our lives. Essentially, nothing is sacred. Even my den has been through two rounds of decorating. I've noticed that while everything else in the house seems to be lighter and brighter with each change, my den becomes darker, danker, more of the brown-light, dry-cough stodginess of a nineteenth-century men's club.

"So," Shirley says, "what's this new case about, the one you've been meeting on so much?"

"Oh, nothing much. Corporate malfeasance, maybe embezzlement." I stop. That part shouldn't have been said. No one knows of my meeting with Armstor, and if Shirley somehow mentions embezzlement in the wrong group, especially in front of Jerry, he'd bore in like the termite he is. She doesn't seem to notice, though.

"I thought you didn't really try cases anymore," she says.

"I don't. But sometimes I'm the babysitter, especially if the client calls me first."

"Babysitter?"

"I hold the client's hand while the real work is done by someone else."

"Holding hands, huh?" Her words tighten my stomach.

"Poor choice of words. The guy calls me and wants me in

61

on the case from the beginning. Jerry's really the one doing all the work... and Ellen." I'm not hungry anymore.

"How is Jerry?"

"Same, same. He's fine. Why?"

"Oh, I guess the last time I saw him, he looked, I don't know, a little sad, maybe. How's his love life?"

"Jesus, Shirley, that's one love life I *don't* want to know about."

"Come on, Winston. We've given up on him long ago." She laughs. "I remember when Carol first met him. 'Shameful waste of good man-flesh,' she'd said."

"That was before her... conversion experience," I say. "Wonder what she'd say now."

Shirley puts a hand over her smile. "She'd try to convert him, first to Christ, then into a heterosexual."

"Go straight. That's never going to happen."

"Don't be so sure. Carol's convincing."

I sense Shirley wants me to ask about the status of her theology and maybe have a conversation about life after death and all that. But I can't.

Carol tells us she "prays without ceasing" for Shirley. But the more Carol prays, the more bad news Shirley gets. I consider taking Carol on. But she's not here, and it'll only bring an abrupt end to the evening with Shirley. And something about this very moment, sitting with her at dinner, the small talk with no agenda, is like a vague memory that tantalizes me. It's not exactly the past, but just enough so that I crave more.

It's unusual for me to be home on Friday, but Paula said something about needing to talk with her father and asked me for bus fare to Cincinnati—to see him for the weekend. I offered a plane ticket, but she turned it down.

A few months after her mother died, her father persuaded her to join him on a tourist safari to Tanzania on the premise of drawing them closer together. Paula and her mother had been nearly inseparable. Her mother would visit from Cincinnati several times a year, sometimes for weeks at a time. After the aneurysm took her life, Paula's father moved on quickly and began to date another woman. While his new-found love angered Paula, I declined to point out the parallel with our own situation.

Eventually, he started calling her more often. He said he knew they weren't as close as she and her mother, but he wanted to spend more time with her. Paula wondered about that. She once told her mother that she and her father had an agnostic relationship. It wasn't good, wasn't bad, it just wasn't.

She was reluctant when her father suggested the Serengeti trip, and that brought on guilt, and the guilt made her do it. He said the safari would be the beginning of a special time in their lives. It didn't work. She thought it a grandiose scheme, a trip to Africa, and she discovered she hated living in a tent in the wild for two weeks. The worst part, though, was that he brought his girlfriend along.

Still, she deeply wanted him to be a part of her life, "woven into my life like a prayer I can call on any time," she'd often tell me. She said it hurt when he couldn't grasp what that meant, and at one point, she thought the conflict she felt over him would drive her mad. I know I'll hear more than I care to when she gets back.

I look across the table at Shirley, and the idea that sitting here, it's like we'd never stopped having dinner together on Fridays grows into a false reality. But it's strange how something once so much a part of your life's routine can disappear for long periods, then suddenly return, behaving as though it never ceased. Still, the fact that everything's changed makes it different, somehow more precious than simple habits. I'd like our time to be special, but I don't know how to make it so. Carol had made dinner at Shirley's request. Then she left, at Shirley's request, so we could be alone.

I worry about being alone and maybe too open with her. Even the babysitting and hand-holding discussion scared me. It might have pointed us toward my infidelity, or worse; she may have concocted this dinner to tell me she was through with chemo and has set sail resigned to fate.

Shirley looks across the table at me. "Winston, I want to say something, and I just want you to listen. All right?"

"Okay," I say, bracing myself. This is her floor, her stage now.

"Our marriage has been a slow-motion separation." She laughs nervously. "Like an iceberg that cracked down the middle somewhere in time and began a slide, melting into the ocean in two different directions. I've gone my way to cancer and certainly an early death."

"Shirley..."

She puts up her hand. I stop. Shirley starts again. "If I could, I'd just put a stop to it. It was the same with you. You had no more choice about your life than I have about my death. I've understood that about you since the first night we held each other. It became a certainty when you were made managing partner. In some ways, it was a promotion, and those on the outside thought you'd made it and reached the top. We both knew it wasn't destiny. It's just where you went, drawn deeper into a life preordained by your father." She took a quick breath.

I try again. "Shirley..."

"I'm okay. I just need a couple more minutes, that's all." She forces a smile through her lips, now pressed together and gone bloodless. "Well," she says, "I've always thought we should admit it when there's an elephant in the room, but we've never been very good at it." She laughs as the color in her face fades, and her forehead knits from the inevitable wave of pain that washes over her. "Well, maybe I can't say much more. But I want you to know that I've understood all along that you've never had a choice in what you did, and I've always known..." she winces and puts both hands on her chest.

I stand up and summon something meaningful from my mind. "I know what you're saying, Shirley. I've always known you understood more than we've ever said. You don't need to say it."

She smiles through the exhaustion that has overrun her in mere seconds. "Good. I'm glad I don't have to explain it to you." She levels her eyes at me. "We're a fine, stubborn pair, aren't we?" she says.

"Yes, we are."

"Don't stop, Winston. Don't stop being that stubborn man. I sense you're going to need that more than you know." All I can do is nod.

We got past it, and here she sits, with me, talking of our relationship as if we were ordinary people just catching up with each other at week's end.

She shakes her head. "I guess I'm just tired. I should probably go to bed. I'm afraid that when I get up, I'll be dizzy."

I lurch from my chair and bump into the table. Nothing tips, but the water and wine splash in their glasses and launch small dollops of liquid onto the white tablecloth. It took less than half an hour for dinner to collapse around us, shaken to the core by chemo, by cancer, by the truth, partial as it was, and the fear of scratching off yet other scabs.

I come around the table and pull back her chair. We move slowly up the stairs. "You holding up?" I ask. She nods. It seems to take forever to get her to the bedroom. "You all right?" I ask twice more. She doesn't reply, but looks up at me once we have her sitting on the edge of the bed. I get her nightgown and robe, lay them on the bed beside her and ask once more, "You all right?" She almost laughs, and I can see her considering an answer. But she only has the strength to say, "I need you to go, Winston, while I get undressed." I leave.

I roll toward the clock and see it's nearly two a.m. Shirley shifts behind me, sliding closer until we're almost touching. We used to take turns snuggling up to the back of one another, spooning in bed. We'd pretend to argue like attorneys about who would be the snuggle-er and who the snuggle-ee. It's childish, embarrassing even, to think about. But it felt good then, and I miss it now.

There was a time when we loved each other deeply. A few years back, I found a stash of letters I'd sent Shirley after she'd dropped out of law school and before we decided to marry. There were maybe a dozen. I was taken by the love and tenderness, the vulnerability in them and the fact they were in my handwriting. It surprised me. At first, I couldn't remember having written them, but slowly, one by one, they returned as if waking out of a deep sleep when awareness creeps back into consciousness. I was a better person then.

She'd torn my name off the bottom of each letter as if she prized what they said but couldn't bear the thought that I had written them. I wondered when she'd done that and who she might have pretended they were from. Still, she'd kept them, love letters, some with poetry from our college days. I've never asked her about it. I just put them back and forgot until now.

That I was easily overwhelmed is something Shirley sensed from the beginning. Every day for more than three decades, I've pushed myself past that feeling, gotten out of bed and gone to work. I swear I won't let us talk about it anymore after tonight. But in the beginning, she encouraged me to let down, let her hold me, heal me. In those days, I took all of her I could get and then clung to the memory of her smell on the way to work.

But as I've said, it all stopped a decade ago or so. I really can't put my finger on why it stopped. Since then, we've grown indifferent to each other. I forced myself deeper into the firm, and she did little but care for the house and occasional volunteer work. Shirley once suggested counseling, but I didn't see the need. We were fine.

Since then, I've had other women in my life, two full-blown affairs, plus a handful of indiscretions. Now, as I lay waiting for the next minute to appear on the face of the clock, my back feels strange, almost naked, and I covet Shirley's frame around me. I imagine she snuggles up to me and matches the form of my body, legs bent to bent legs. But she doesn't move.

I shut my eyes, and Paula's naked form appears. I often try to imagine Paula when I look at Shirley. But they can't coexist. They flow around each other like water and oil, each carving her own liquid path.

I roll back toward Shirley. I can't remember the last time we turned out the light after laughing about something. We haven't made love since she went on the stronger chemo. I could get up but decide I'll just lay here until morning, even if I never sleep.

Somehow, being close to her helps me put off thinking about Armstor. I checked my email when I got home, and there he was, asking that we meet tomorrow. I shot back a note agreeing to see him. Dad is being taken in for tests in the afternoon, and I suggested we meet at his house at two.

I just need to confront Armstor and put his illegal, unethical, dangerous request behind me.

Chapter 8

On Saturday, I leave the office before noon and drive north along Lakeshore Drive until it turns into Sheridan Road. Downtown Chicago slowly dissipates as I wind along the lake into the upscale homes of Evanston. Most are between eighty and a hundred years of age but generally well cared for. Dad's is on the right-hand side of a sharp turn in the road. A heavy gate closes the street that used to run straight through the neighborhood before I was born. The two-story Tudor has three gables facing the short, private street. Each is overgrown with ivy that hides the sad shape of brick and mortar beneath it. Dad's home is on the slide, and I'm sure the neighbors can't stand it. Jerry once examined the exterior and said a mason could put several kids through college on the tuck and point job the place needs. I'm sure I don't know.

The yard, such as it is, was never big enough to throw a ball around in, never mind it wasn't allowed; it might hurt the chiseled shrubbery that now stretches and droops in several unruly directions. Probably a month's work to make even that presentable.

From three sides, it doesn't really matter how the place looks since a six-foot red brick fence encircles the property. The trouble is that the brick is in worse shape than the house. As I pull into the driveway, I'm once more struck by the former elegance, the power and position lost in decay. Maybe

Dad was right to put his trust in Jerry. I haven't taken care of him or his property.

I remember when it was the finest house in the neighborhood. Now, the lawn service does less and less as it seems no one any longer cares what the grounds look like. Its stateliness still shows through the faded paint on the high stucco panels, and even the black moss that hangs under the eaves can't blot out the fact this was the home of someone once important. I pause, taking in the decayed exterior.

I let myself in with the key Shirley gave me over a year ago. "You need to stop and see him more often, Winston. He won't be with us forever," she'd said. I don't actually remember whether I've been here in the past year or not. But I know the aide has taken him to the doctor this morning, and the house is empty.

I step inside the huge foyer and stare around at the unlit room, then up at the arcing ceiling. The stairs are in front of me, its banister dark and threatening with the pineapple newel post and what I'd always thought was a gargoyle carved in it. Shirley had scoffed at me. It was only a pineapple, she'd said. What could she know? After all, I was the one who sat on the bench beneath the antique coat tree as a boy and stared at it more times than I care to remember. And each time, it stared back. It stares at me now.

I consider going up the wide, curved stairway, but remember that my father moved his bedroom to the back of the house on the main floor and sealed off the second floor at the top of the stairs. He'd wanted to move to the library, but Shirley convinced him it would be better to leave it "a place you can visit, Father, a change of scenery." Instead, she'd talked him into converting the den from where he could look out its window into the conservatory, the paint peeling off its metal frame or wheel himself around through the French doors into its airy light.

I walk through the parlor, the dining room and into the kitchen... smells of age and antiseptic. I go back through the parlor to the den with its crypt-like door, arched at the top, as the feeling comes over me again: the dread of living, of breathing, of being in this place. I steel myself and push open the door. The room is dim. The smell of urine surges in my nostrils and draws my eyes to the oversized hospital bed. Even with the space it takes up, the room's denliness holds its own, though I can't see clearly. I never liked it in here, where Dad would puff and chew cigars as he read late into the night. By the time I left home, I understood he was as much avoiding Mom and me as he was working. I can almost see him sitting behind the dark walnut desk, smoke encircling his head, his thick hair holding the cigar smell long after he'd left the room. That smell covered everything. Even my mother's presence was overwhelmed by it.

Whenever I'd stick my head in, he'd puff harder as if to disappear in the cloud. I remember feeling isolated like I was folding inward, turning inside myself, shrinking from the edges like the troublesome spot in a cheap cigar where somewhere in the middle it starts to burn internally, the foul, blackened tar imploding on itself, hardening like a fossil unless relit around the wrapper, sucking the orange coal back into life around the edges.

"Hello... Anyone home?" a small but whiny voice calls out from the distance. Armstor has arrived.

"Yes, I'm in the den," I yell. "Just a minute." I pretend to cast my feelings into the room and snatch the door shut. It's a silly act.

When I reach the foyer, Armstor is taking off his sports coat. He hooks it over the coat rack as if he lives here. A small leather satchel lies at his feet. I look at my watch. "You're early. It's only one-thirty."

"Better early than late." He looks around. "Nice. At least it was once upon a time. The location's good, but you've kind of let this place go. Can't imagine your father can't afford to take care of it."

"Money's not the problem. He isn't going to be here long. He needs help twenty-four hours a day now, and we'll be moving him to a home soon."

Armstor shakes his head. "Still, it's a shame."

I know enough to feel guilty about my lack of attention to the house and, by extension, to my father, but I can't let it bother me with Armstor here. "Okay, Sam. We're here now. Let's get something straight..."

"You know why I called you in the first place, why I asked you to be my attorney?"

"No, well, I assume you know about our firm, how we've, well, we have a certain reputation when it comes to defending corporate officers."

Armstor smiles. "I was only the controller, not a senior officer." He gestures to the stairway, and I nod. He sits down on the steps. "I'm afraid that's not it, Winston. Didn't know a thing about the firm's reputation. I spent some time reviewing State Bar ethics cases. I found you there and read about the Molotelco, shall we say, situation. I was looking for someone with grit, the kind of grit it would take to push the envelope, maybe even tear it open. That's where I found you, right here in the middle of an otherwise spotless firm."

My hands feel oddly out of place, and I fidget for a moment before getting them under control. I've come to accept Molotelco as a scarlet *E* on the breast of my ethical character. "That's an unlikely source for recommendations," I say.

He laughs. "I suppose. But as I said, I was looking for grit. I think you have it. I know it's not conventional, but I'm not looking for a conventional man. I've got most things covered, you know, but I need your help."

"All I know is that the Justice Department is worried about what they haven't found yet and, yes, that made me wonder..."

"They should worry," Armstor says. "I was pretty thorough, blotting out the trail I'd left. You ever heard the name Matthew Gardener?" I shake my head. "Matt was part of the

Aronson Consulting group that broke up after all those accounting scandals a few years ago. Matt himself had signed off false statements. Then he'd shredded documents despite an SEC order to the contrary. But he was caught.

"When Aronson folded, Matt was indicted, but all charges were dropped in a plea agreement that included a stipulation he would never again work as a public accountant. He was through.

"But he's never really gone away, just underground. He once told me that, just when he thought his life was ruined, he was in greater demand than ever. 'Company executives are coming out of the woodwork,' he said. Matt skulked behind the scenes on behalf of several company officers in at least three major corporate scandals. He'd even joked about the reason he was in such demand: 'It takes one to know one.' I once asked him how a senior accountant in a major firm could move so completely to what Matt himself described as 'the dark side.' Matt's only answer was, 'We are all capable of much, so very much.' Then he'd laughed."

"What's this got to do with me?"

"Not much, really. The heavy lifting's done. I got to know some of the technology staff at RoneCraft. I put Matt onto one of the network guys in the IT department, a guy I knew wasn't happy with the company. Matt had the guy erase things from my computer, all the servers, and the network. I'd kept a list of things, specific folders, where everything was."

"You get it all?"

"As much as we can be sure of anything today, we did. It cost me two hundred grand to get the network administrator to delete and overwrite the data. By the time the feds got there with the court order, they didn't find much."

"When did you do this?"

"Almost three months before they charged me. I was getting nervous and had everything erased."

"What about the computer forensics team? I'm sure Justice has them on the hunt. When they get done examining the hardware and software, they'll see things have been tampered with."

"Look, I know, Winston. But we've done everything we can. All the things the geeks look for, we've covered. They may find that someone's been messing around with the systems, but my network buddy was from India, and he quit RoneCraft and went home. I don't think we'll see him again."

"So why do you need me?"

Armstor sighed. "Well, it's Matt. I made a deal with the bastard, and now he's trying to hold me up for more."

"How much?"

"I originally paid him two-fifty. Now he wants another two-fifty. I got it, you know, but I have to make sure he doesn't just turn around and ask for more. Again."

"But I'm just a lawyer," I say. "You want me to threaten him with a lawsuit? Maybe beat him to death with a subpoena?"

Armstor laughs, although I'd never meant to be funny. "No, no. Nothing like that. Listen, all I need from you is to have you deliver the final payment and have a talk with him. Tell him how much we all have to lose if he keeps messing with me. Reason with him, you know, tell him to move on, live to fight another day, that sort of thing."

"And for that one conversation, which you've already scripted, I get millions? Seems excessive, even to a lawyer."

"Well, there might be more to do later. I just need an ally in this, Winston. I thought I could handle it myself, but frankly, it's starting to get to me. I'm not built to handle the pressure. I didn't set out in the beginning to do it all. Just took one step at a time. I thought the first acquisition was going to cost me my job. When the second came along, I panicked and decided to do something to take care of myself if things blew up. When more acquisitions came my way, I just kept doing what I'd done before, and eventually, I am where I am."

I consider just how pathetic he looks. It could be true. He goes on, "I can't trust my wife, can't trust your partners, especially the zealous one, the guy could pry information and money out of concrete. And your accounting specialist... how long do you think she'll be able to keep quiet about what I did? Hell, I don't have anyone, and it wouldn't be any different with another firm. That's why I came to you after I read about Molotelco. It seemed to me that you were just doing what was practical given the circumstances." He leans toward me. "So, will you do it? Will you talk to Matt? I've got the money here, with me." He picks up the small leather briefbag. "Two-fifty." He reaches into his pocket and pulls out a folded paper. "And here, here's a wire from my bank in Zurich. It's for you if you'll do this for me. Half a million. No questions, no stipulations. There'll be more once I clear the last legal hurdle." He puts the bag and the check in one hand and holds them out to me. I don't take them, so he sets both on the bottom step of the stairs. "I'll leave this with you if you'd like to think about it. I trust you won't take it and run."

Now would be the time to tell him to get out...tell him to take his money, the wire, and get the hell out of my father's house. I reach down and pick up the bag. "Just what would I do with this?"

"Take it to Matt. Today."

"You're pretty confident I'll do this."

"I had the appointment myself, and if you don't, then I'll have to. But I want your help."

"Where are you meeting him?"

"Chesterton, Indiana. Dunes State Park. Its..."

"I know where it is, just off the interstate. What time?"

"Late today. Between six and eight, before dark. He'll come in by boat from Lake Michigan and meet you at the shelter where the main parking lot is. I've met him there before. We usually walk off down the shoreline a ways and climb a sand dune to do our business."

I close my eyes. I've never been all that good at decision-making. Things have a way of overtaking me, especially in the past couple of years, as I've begun to spin out of control.

We actually decide very few things for ourselves. Events defy the conventional wisdom that we can control our own lives—we make plans and follow through on those plans—when, in reality, we control little or nothing. Even Armstor, as sleazy as I find him, started with nothing greater than an ethical lapse driven by fear for his future. Then he kept on going, on a grander scale, until here we stand, him bribing me in the face of going to prison.

"Six o'clock, you say?" I look at my watch.

"Yes. But maybe as late as eight. He'll be coming down from Milwaukee, and it depends on the water. He's got a hell of a boat, but the lake can get rough, and then he'd need to slow down."

I nod. "Okay," I say. "I'll meet him, have a talk."

Armstor stands up and takes my hand. He looks as if he might cry, and I find that and the moist handshake both surprising and pathetic. "Thanks, thank you. You won't regret it, Winston. This is a relief to me. You can't imagine. Look," he hands me the check, "take this. You take it, and we've got a deal." He holds out his hand. I take the money as what I've done runs through my mind until I feel his palm sweating in mine.

Once Armstor is gone, I look around inside the house. I haven't been past the foyer for over a year. The place was built when rooms were formal and separate and grand, big and dark, with six and ten panel oak doors stained deeply and varnished several times, now old enough to have yellowed somewhat.

Double doors between the kitchen and dining room were meant to be closed when company attended. In the corner of the dining room, a curious, smallish archway, rough plastered, a tunnel to shuttle food from the kitchen to polite company gathered to break bread. I remember first-time guests remarking how quaint it was, ignoring its antebellum flavor. The arch is about eight feet long and not quite six at its peak. It runs alongside the back wall of the pantry. Inside, a small half-moon cove holds a curved sofa table. Mother kept it covered with a silk cloth that hung to the floor. Up until I was ten, I could fit beneath it, sitting for hours in the muted light, pretending it was a fort.

After Mom died, Dad put a blackened bronze statue of a Negro child on it. The boy sat with one leg over the edge, a fishing line tied in a bow to his big toe lest there be any doubt about the architectural meaning of the narrow passageway through which house slaves would pass, ducking their heads in high domesticity to deliver vast spreads of food that were seldom fully consumed by the respectable people my parents had become. It was ugly and out of place in suburban Chicago. But one had to admit the perfection of the stereotype.

I look at my watch and realize I need to be on the road. I consider this step. By itself, it's not the worst thing I've done. But I recognize the dichotomy of deliberately taking the slippery slope while knowing better.

It takes just over an hour to reach Chesterton, Indiana, from downtown Chicago. I pull off Interstate ninety, drive into Dunes State Park and park the Humvee next to the only other car in the lot. It's exactly six o'clock. I put the leather bag in the pocket of my overcoat. I haven't looked inside, afraid of the cash Armstor said was there. It grows heavy as I walk down to the shore of Lake Michigan, look east toward Buffalo City, then back toward Chicago. The power plants in the distance toward Gary sit at the edge of the lake and billow smoke like a scene from a post-Armageddon movie.

I can see two people climbing the dunes to the east, maybe half a mile away. Otherwise, the park is empty. I turn to the west and walk a quarter mile, then climb one of the dunes, the soft, damp sand giving way under each step until I find a level spot and sit down.

I'm alone long enough to hear the water lapping on the shore thirty yards away. The waves are lake waves, but still noisy and larger than they should be. The sound of a distant engine surges, then retreats, then surges again. I look out across the lake, where a single boat, still far out in the water, is cutting its way toward me. The sound comes and goes as the boat rises and falls in the water. Only a cream-colored convertible top is visible. In a few minutes, I can see the hull and the top of what looks like a highly polished, antique wooden boat. It's a runabout, probably a twenty-four-footer, and nicely restored.

My father once nearly bought one like it. He said it reminded him of growing up along the lake in Wisconsin, near Cedarburg, where boats like this were common among the moneyed crowd. When I was a teenager, he came close to getting a very nice one. We looked at it on three different Sundays, and I had the chance to steer it once, fell completely in love and could hardly wait to own it. But on the third viewing, Dad brought along a dealer who knew the antique boat business. He told my father the boat wasn't an antique, that it was of modern construction through and through, and that, while it was well made, it couldn't be over five years old. Dad never went back and never talked about it again.

I look up, fully expecting to be filled with admiration at the approaching boat. But as it draws nearer, I have a memory, just for a moment, of setting aside my anger at not getting that boat and taking in the disappointment on my father's face at the dealer's revelation.

The classic wood-hulled runabout, stained a medium oak and varnished to a high gloss, makes its way toward me. I grow suspect of its authenticity, as if, undeserving of the genuine article, its owner manufactured a skin and stretched it over the general deceit of a life fueled with unspoken disappointment.

Within a few minutes, the boat stops probably fifty yards from land. A man stands up and slides a rubber dingy over the side. He slips into it and paddles to land, beaches the craft, straightens up and waves at me. I wave back.

It takes him no time to climb the dunes. He's lean, robust, and has the pre-middle-aged handsomeness I once fancied I had. It's only May, but his face beams with an August tan. He reaches out his hand as he approaches.

"Hello. You Winston?"

"Yes," I say, standing up.

"Sam said you'd be here. Matt Gardener's my name, but I'm sure you know that. Can I see some ID?"

The request surprises me. I brush sand off my seat and take out my wallet. He stares at my license for what seems too long. A hint of contempt rises through the curl on his upper lip. He hands my wallet back and stands still, as if waiting. Finally, he takes out his own wallet and hands me his license. I take it, not understanding at first, but then realize what I'm doing. Of course, I need to know exactly who he is. We're in the process of committing a crime, stranger to stranger, and if either of us makes a mistake, well...

"Satisfied?" he asks.

"Yes, I am. But then, as you saw, I was probably satisfied without looking at this."

"It's a formality, you know," he says, holding his license up. "Could be fake." I must have some kind of look on my face. He laughs. "Just kidding. Now, let's get down to business. You bring the money?"

He stares at the bulge in my overcoat. I put my hand in the pocket and feel the brushed leather warming to my touch. I could leave. I should leave. I can't imagine how I let myself get here. Armstor could have delivered this himself. I remember the wire transfer draft in my pocket and hand Gardener the pouch. He opens it, and I watch as he sorts through several packs of thousand-dollar bills. He nods. "It's all here, I guess."

I don't know why I've come. It seems too simple and too wrong at the same time. "That it?" I ask.

He smiles. "That's it, unless you want to give me another hundred grand." I knit my brow. "No, guess you don't, huh?"

"Listen," I say. "Sam told me this is the second installment; one he hadn't planned for."

Gardener looks amused and eyes me deliberately, top to bottom. "Heh, so you're his enforcer?"

"No, just his attorney." From somewhere, I summon the man I once was. "But I'll tell you right now that this is the last of it. Nothing more. He had a deal, paid you, and now you want more. This time, it's shame on you. Next time, it would be shame on us. So, we're through now. You've been paid, well paid."

He stops smiling. "Don't give me that honor among thieves routine, my friend. Sam can still go to jail over this. And you probably could, too."

I laugh. "He's done paying you. Period. And as for me, you'd be surprised how little I care what happens. Look, he asked me to talk to you. I'm not interested in honor or threats. If you want to stay under the radar, you'll take this payment and close the file."

"Only a goddamn lawyer would tell me to 'close the file.'"

"Think we're kidding?"

He studies my face carefully even though I've no idea what he sees. "Okay," he says. "It's interesting, though, to discover I've got more to lose than either of you."

"So you're in agreement?" I stare at him. The pause is calculated to make him uncomfortable while I focus on not caring what happens, just as I'd said.

"Well, sir, we do understand each other. It's done, then."

He touches his hand to his eyebrow in salute, turns and walks down the dune to the dingy. I watch as he rows back to his boat. The engine starts. He waves once more and turns, heads into open water.

The sun is low to the west and strikes the side of my face. *You okay, Winston?* I hear myself say. I jump and shake my head, then laugh toward where Matt, his boat, and the sound of the motor disappear into the horizon. *Yes, yeah,* I say. *I'm fine.*

I sit down again in the late afternoon shadows and listen to the waves. The park is empty as the last glint of sunlight leaves the water in front of me. The sand turns from yellow to grey and matches the sunless water. They are one, except that the lake still moves. I'm pulled from my trance by a shiver. Fear, I think, comes back to haunt me. There's no controlling it as it comes and goes at will, rifling through my body and mind. Is it fear over what I've done? I can think clearly about this deception. I could look at myself in the mirror, in fact, and feel nothing. Besides, these episodes were with me before all this began.

The park is deserted, and only my yellow Humvee can be seen in the descending shadow of night. It's cold in the May dusk, and I shiver again. I look at my watch, then pull out my cell phone and call the hotel. Paula doesn't answer, and I remember she's gone this weekend. I have nowhere to go but home.

Chapter 9

I never need an alarm on Sunday. Carol is there before either Shirley or I wake up. Even when Shirley's sleep is tenuous, it seems that Carol somehow finds her way into our house during one of the brief rem cycles Shirley does sink into.

But even without her, I get up early on Sunday morning. I'd rather sleep in, but my childhood returns and my mother's face implores me to go to church with her, something my father never did and another thing I envied about him. I always did go with her, even when I came home from college, even if it meant I was just getting home from an all-night party.

It's eight o'clock, and Carol has already been to the six-a.m. service in whatever true-way tabernacle she's attending now. Changing churches substitutes for changing wardrobes. I'm certain her husband is grateful, since it doesn't cost as much as a new wardrobe. He'd once laid down the law that nothing he earned would be given to a church, but if she went to work, she could give her whole goddamn check for all he cared. It was the only thing I admired about him. Randolph Webster held a PhD in American History. It seems he'd once been on the fast track to tenure at the University of Virginia. Then he published a series of research articles where some of his documented "sources" turned out to be claptrap he'd dreamt up. A fool, a sham, he moved to Chicago and found ready work in the community college circuit, but only as an adjunct since, in academic circles, he was anathema.

He also found Carol in the Shedd Aquarium one blustery March afternoon. She was recovering from her second divorce, and he, being not unperceptive, picked up on her needy nature, the desperation to talk with someone. He had the time to listen. And he did listen, so I never had much sympathy for him when he complained about her incessant talk. Luckily, a dozen or so years after they were married, she found Jesus and didn't need his ear much after that. With Shirley having now become Carol's major project in life, he seems off the hook entirely, and I often envy him for it.

I roll slowly across our king-sized bed, fully expecting to see Shirley staring at me. Instead, she remains asleep, and I recognize it's deeper than I've seen it in a long time. I edge away and slip over my side of the bed and into the bathroom. Once I'm dressed, I stop by the doorway and look back. She lies on her side in the shadows of the light through the window blinds. The cream-colored comforter takes on a grey cast and bulks up the silhouette of her thin frame. The curves of her body are gone, hidden under the covers and emaciating away day by day as her hips collapse. In her better moments, she jokes that by morphing into a pencil, she'll be a runway model in the next life. Carol never sees the humor and launches into a long, colorful description of heaven that is either hopeful encouragement or evangelical nonsense. You might guess which view I take.

But at this moment, Shirley's sleep is a rare gift. It's a natural sleep. Not the chemo-induced coma, the sleep of the dead that I often feel chilling next to me in bed. I wonder, at times like this, what she thinks of impending death. How can the mind absorb this reality in the midst of pain so strong as to mark death's inevitability? But the sicker she is, the less she cares, I guess.

I can't look at her head sticking out of the covers. Her hair is beginning to fall out again, and I expect that it will be complete in just a few days. I have an urge to go over to her and tuck her in, but I can't because it might wake her.

Instead, I stand by the door and ignore the decorating magazines scattered on the floor. I try to burn this memory in my mind: the soft light and shadows, the room, cool from careful control: not too warm because it makes her restless, not too cool because her body temperature drops like a stone in water. This perfect environmental balance in our sanctuary has just the right elements to let her sleep in satisfaction, if only for one more morning.

It occurs to me there is only this one morning, only the here and now. The past is stored away, the future unknown. Time moves in equal measure with no regard to events inside it. We sink toward death. We take ever larger steps toward moral bankruptcy. We multiply our wrongdoing in deliberate acts. We cling more tightly to Jesus even as our doubts about him grow. Time, however, merely passes.

I wonder if she hears me thinking like this. I've heard it said that people under extraordinary conditions sometimes develop facilities the rest of us, the less focused, can't ever have. I hope she does read my mind. I don't think I can ever cross the eroded chasm we have between us to actually talk of this.

I gird myself. Besides, I think it's nonsense.

I slip out the door to the smell of pancakes rising from downstairs. For some reason, Carol works up a farmer's breakfast each Sunday. Not that I complain.

"Good morning, Winston," she says. "Can you watch the griddle? I'm going up to help Shirley."

"She's asleep," I say.

Carol looks up from the steaming white puddles she's just dropped on the griddle. "Sleeping? Really sleeping?"

"Yes. The kind of sleep I haven't seen in months."

Carol smiles. "Praise the Lord. I've been praying for this, just a little reprieve now and then from the..."

"I know. You've told me that before."

"And she's getting it?"

"Yes."

She smiles and raises both her eyebrows. "See? It worked. God is so good, Winston."

"I wouldn't know about that, and I wouldn't go up to see her just now, or you'll wake her, and all of God's good work will be for naught."

"Tch, tch, tch. Don't be such a spoil sport on the Lord's Day."

"Look, Carol, let's just be civil to each other. Let's do it for Shirley's sake, so she doesn't feel the vibrations of our mutual dislike. It'll ruin her morning."

"I didn't think you knew that people could be that sensitive, Winston. You're certainly not."

"I didn't say I was."

Carol flips the pancakes. "All right. Let's be friends today." She waits a moment, then deftly flips one pancake on top of another until all six are in a stack. She puts a finger on top of the stack, sweeps the spatula under it and turns it over onto a plate beside the stove.

"You do that just like my mother did," I hear myself say.

Carol pauses and takes in my face while caution covers hers. "Do what?"

"Flip pancakes." I start to laugh.

"Well, I'm not sure, but I think I hear approval in your voice."

"It is, I do, I mean, I used to watch her. It made me hungrier the longer I watched."

"I thought you had a cook and servants when you were a kid."

"Not on Sundays. Mother did all the cooking on Sundays unless we went out to eat."

"And how often was that?"

I laugh. "Okay, okay, it was more than half the time. But she did it as a reward for going to church with her."

Carol's eyes flash toward me, then away. "Church?"

84

"Yeah," I answer. "Mass. Church." The conversation has already gone further than I want it to.

Carol ladles six more puddles on the griddle. She sets down the batter and dusts off her hands. "Well-well, at least then you know where to look when it's time." I don't answer her but dread the certainty she'll not let it go. "So, Winston. Were you never persuaded by any of it?"

"Theology was interesting. Religion wasn't."

"Hmmm. So, it was a little intellectual stimulation you were after? That and breakfast?"

"I wasn't *after* anything. I did it as a favor to my mother."

"A favor?"

"Yes. She didn't want to go alone, so I went with her. Sometimes, we'd go back in the evenings for just a quiet sit in the pews where I'd watch her pray."

"And your father?"

"He never went."

Carol nodded as she flipped the pancakes. They were over-brown, and she turned the dial on the griddle. "So if it was theology only, then at least at one point in your life you got the moral groundings."

"Moral groundings?"

"That's what I said, Winston. *Moral groundings.*"

"What are you getting at, Carol?"

"What do you think I'm getting at?"

"I'm sure I don't know."

"I'm sure you do."

I watch as Carol flips the pancakes again and puts them on the stack. She peels off three with her fingers and tosses them onto a plate. She points to it and nods.

"I'm not hungry," I say. I turn away and start for the garage.

"She's not a fool, Winston." I stop. "She knows, you know. Oh, not the details, not exactly who it is, but she knows the type."

I spin around. "Type? What type?"

Carol jerks her head back. "Well-well. I guess it's more

than a fling. Don't tell me you actually care for this woman."

I walk toward her, half whispering, "I don't know what you mean, *Carol*, since there's nothing to whatever is going on in your head."

"Then what's this?" She holds up an envelope. "I found it under the Sunday paper when I came in, thought it was the bill." She hands the opened envelope to me and stands back, folding her arms. It was addressed only "To Winston," written in the perfect cursive script found on the walls of elementary schools. I open it and pull out a three-by-five card with a phone number and the words, "Call me after 10 p.m." It was signed by Meghan Armstor. I can't decide if Carol thinks the look on my face is guilt or just the surprise I feel. I gather myself and hold the card in the air.

"This is from a client, the Armstors. I *represent* them."

"Really. Well, judging from what I could tell, it's from *half* your client, the female half."

"I don't have to explain this to you."

"No. But you owe Shirley. I mean, even if you're telling the truth—about this one—it doesn't get you off the hook. There *is* something going on... some woman somewhere."

"That's a lie."

"Add it all up, Winston. On Fridays, you're gone until late. When you come home, you're always fresh and clean."

"What?"

"Shirley's told me. You get in bed after midnight every Friday, smelling like a fresh shower. And you don't take one when you get home. Look, I know you've done this before, over the years. Shirley knows it, too."

"And you're what, defending her honor?"

"Dignity, Winston, her dignity."

"And just how are you doing that by accusing me?"

Carol leans back against the counter and sighs. "Well, you're right about that. It doesn't help her at all unless *you* decide to straighten up."

"Or until you butt out of our lives."

She levels her eyes at me. "She deserves better, Winston. Didn't you get any of that in your so-called theology lessons?"

"Damnit, Carol..."

"Don't you damn anything," she says.

"Well, I'll be. You *can* swear."

"I..."

"What's going on here?" Shirley stands in the kitchen doorway. I watch as she floats toward us, ghost-like in her pale skin and grey housecoat. They blend together in a single being. I lower my eyes, but not before I see Carol do the same.

"You two could wake the dead. And in my case, that's entirely possible." Shirley crosses to the marble island and leans on a stool. "Okay, Winston. Let's see the note." I hand it to her and want to speak but don't since I can't think of what to say. Shirley studies it for a moment, then looks up at Carol. "It's true, Carol. This is one of Winston's clients. Margaret told me about it the other day. Her husband was in the news not too long ago, and he's come to the firm for help."

Carol makes eye contact with Shirley. I can see the temptation growing inside her, the need to say it, that it doesn't matter if Meghan Armstor is a client because the real point is that he, me, Winston, is dirty nonetheless. But she can't, not with me here and with Shirley defending me. Carol's seen this before. She's heard us arguing and jumped in on Shirley's side only to feel Shirley turn on her.

I stare at Carol until she looks at me. "I've had enough of this nonsense." I turn to Shirley. "I'm going to the office. Don't worry about dinner." Neither woman stops me as I snatch my keys off the counter and make my exit.

The office is dark and only the safety lights are on in the hallways. The office is warm, with the air conditioning shut down on Sundays. Stale, sweaty air resists my movement and makes me feel heavy and slow. I can feel my underarms staining my shirt like the stain of conscience that envelops me. On one level, it bothers me how easily I lie. But I've lied for so long that even when I tell the truth, it doesn't sound true. I have just come as close to being fully exposed for what I am as ever.

It shouldn't matter whether my infidelity is specifically known. But it does, if only because the lack of specifics lets Shirley decide what to believe. I'm sure, and I worry, that once laid out on the altar of my misdeeds, they will be larger than life, maybe even more than I can bear.

The way things are, I know I should break it off with Paula. But I don't want to and have made my peace with the knowledge that the appetite for avarice, once tasted, is as insatiable as a rogue tiger's need for human flesh.

And still, if I wanted to, could I not simply *choose* to be different?

I look at the clock. It is now ten thirty. I fondle the card with Meghan Armstor's number on it. I shouldn't call her, but then again, my curiosity leaves me no choice.

"Hello?" The voice is clearly hers, but she sounds as if she'd been asleep.

"Oh, ah, this is Winston Williamsen, returning your call. I hope I didn't wake you."

"Well, you did, but then I asked you to call me. You got the note then?"

"Yes. But why didn't you just leave a message on my voice-mail?"

"Because I really wanted to talk to you this morning. It's easier when Sammy's on the golf course."

"Well, if this is a bad time..."

"No, no. I'm on my cell, in my bedroom." She pauses for my response, but I give her none. "Sammy's in his own room. We have separate bedrooms." She pauses again, and while my curiosity is peaked, I remember the hard look on her face at that first meeting in my office. I remain silent.

"Anyway," she goes on, "what I really wanted was to talk with you privately."

"We can do it on the phone," I answer.

"Okay. I'd rather not. But here goes. Sammy's up to something."

"Up to something? Up to what?" I worry but hold my voice steady.

"I don't know for certain, but he's seeing another attorney, I think."

"What?"

"Yes. I think so. I took a call the other day. When he wouldn't give me his name, I asked what it was about. All he said was that it was a legal matter and that he'd call back."

"It might have been my partner, Jerry."

"No. The voice was nasally, and the man seemed nervous."

"Okay, it's not Jerry."

"No, I didn't think so. Winston, are you sure we can't meet somewhere?"

"Do you have anything more?"

"No, but..."

"Well, then, let me look into it. I'm assuming you don't want to ask your husband about it?"

"No. But something's going on."

"It might have just been the press sniffing around."

"Well, Sammy fidgets. Not like he normally does, but nearly all the time, anytime he sits down. It's getting on my nerves."

I nod but then realize she's waiting. "Well, he's under indictment. So don't take the fidgeting as anything more than that. But I'll look into it."

"Can we meet?"

"I'll call you."

"When?"

"I don't know yet."

"Should I... should I get my own attorney?" It occurs to

me that Meghan has a plan, and it doesn't include Samuel Armstor in the long run.

"No. Or do whatever you want. But I wouldn't, not based on what you've told me so far."

"To you, it might not be much. But I know Sammy."

"Okay," I say, "you sit tight until I get back with you. Now, whenever we meet, you need to act as if we didn't talk. You can do that?"

"Yes. I think so."

"Good. Remember, sit tight." I hang up the phone. Nothing has happened, I tell myself. My bowel feels light. "Butterflies," I say. I already know I'll do nothing to follow up on this. Samuel's my client, not his wife. And regardless of my own mental state, hers is not to be relied on. The room seems to darken.

"Nonsense," I say.

Chapter 10

For the past two months, I've largely ignored the Armstor case. I busy myself with Paula and sitting in my office, finding things for Margaret to do. It's not all that easy. She has the capacity of a draft horse and the speed of an Arabian. There are cases passing through the firm, and I review them or pretend to while assuring our billing system is working. There's value in that, I guess.

But today, we have the first real hearing on Armstor. Jerry has talked Collier Clark into a pre-court discussion, hoping to pique his interest in cutting our client a deal. I am to study the file until nine, and then we'll meet the Armstors at Clark's office.

Samuel has only called me once since I met with Matt. He said things seemed settled for now and assured me he'd be in touch about our separate arrangement. But he's never called since, and I've found relief in that, even when every nerve in my body tells me to be concerned.

I do dread seeing Meghan. Based on her unstable call and the fact I don't really want to discover what trouble might be brewing, I've done nothing to respond. But I'm not sure what there is to do, and I never did call her back.

Margaret finally prods me out of the office ten minutes after Jerry has left, and I decide to walk the six blocks north to the Sextant Building. July has been humid, and the beginning of August didn't change that. The dewpoint has been over seventy for twelve days in a row. The breeze off Lake Michigan died in the heat. By the time I sit down in the waiting room next to Jerry, my face is shiny.

I acknowledge Sam, but we don't shake hands. Meghan looks at me with the eyes of a puppy about to be drowned, and I force myself to look away, just as I've ignored her calls. I study Armstor as he fidgets directly across from me in the waiting room on the sixteenth floor of the opulent Sextant Building. The surplus metal chairs and the grey metal coffee table strewn with bent and torn magazines belie the marble floors and scattered Persian rugs. Over-built for the market by unbridled egos in the seventies, the Sextant Building stood nearly empty over two decades as successive owners purchased it at increasing discounts until it was cheap enough to cash flow on rent from the federal government.

The sad furniture stands in stark contrast to the floors, the walls and the permanent wall tapestries, the slightest of which only further cheapens the furniture brought from storage to finish offices for a dozen federal prosecutors. While meant to be temporary offices, they've been here for over four years, and I should be happy with this uncharacteristic frugality. It just tempts my depression further. The federal courtrooms are on the bottom three floors.

I spy a security camera in the corner of the ceiling and imagine Collier Clark on the viewing side of a TV screen conducting his own wingless fly experiment. I look back at Armstor and decide he just looks guilty all the time. To make matters worse, Meghan is right about the increased fidgeting. And even she has difficulty sitting still. Twice, I make eye contact with her but decide to avoid it because she seems too anxious and has an urgent look to say something.

Jerry sits ramrod straight while still relaxed as he quietly reviews the file. How he does that is a mystery that makes me angry. I can't tell how I might look, but I try not to imagine the worst about myself.

Jerry looks up just before I hear Collier Clark approaching from down the hall behind me. I can tell it's him by the way Jerry smiles, and from the tok, tok, tok of tasseled, leather-heeled loafers on the marble floor, its upper-middle-class sound brought low by the poor white trash jingling of too much loose change, rattling in a pocket by a nervous hand trying to outgrow the boyhood pleasure of pocket pool. Clark has always been a complex composite of a man. Soon, I hear that nasally voice.

"Hello, Jerry. It's nice to see you."

Jerry has already stood and, with his classic Jerry smile, reaches out his hand. "Collier," he says. Clark tries to look like Jerry. He has the clothes, the hair gel, and the practiced demeanor. But it comes off as smallish and sweaty. He half reminds me of Armstor. Clark is maybe all of thirty-five, lean but lacking Jerry's athleticism. His dark blue suit stays in straight lines when he moves, and it shimmers in the light. His jet-black hair waves backward from a rounded forehead and a long, hooking nose that, with his adenoids out, could deepen his voice.

Jerry swings one arm toward the Armstors. "Mr. Clark, this is Samuel Armstor and his wife, Meghan." Armstor quits squirming, and looks up from his chair as if he doesn't care. Too nonchalant, I think.

"How do you do, sir." He nods toward Meghan. "Mrs. Armstor." Clark bows slightly at the waist but offers no hand. His voice belies the shiny suit he wears as he hisses, "Missus Armstor." I decide it gives him time to drink the draught of glamour she gives off at first impression. She wears a light brown skirt with a matching jacket and a silk mock turtleneck sweater underneath. Her lipstick and makeup are muted but flawless. Clark notices her white cotton hose, the kind a young girl would wear. The skirt comes smartly down to the bottom of her calves. There's something sensual in her fresh innocence. She looks up at him, and he smiles. Her mouth hardens in return, and lines flash on her forehead, too deep for her age. She looks away. The reaction seems to bother him. Still, here she is, looking just as she should look. He finally turns to me. "Hello, Winston. I wasn't sure you'd be here."

"Wild horses couldn't keep me away," I lie.

Clark leads us to a windowless conference room somewhere in the middle of the building. Even here, the duality of excess mixes with the poverty of make-shift office fixtures. The oversized metal table is substantial and smooth, but the paint has flecked away near the edges. I imagine my father sitting at a table like this just after the war, lawyering his way to respectability while my generation lawyers its way to disrepute.

Clark hurries us into chairs. "Well, here we are now. Jerry, this meeting was at your request, so I'll just turn it over to you."

Jerry leans forward, his arms open on the table. "Thank you. The reason we're here is because our client may be of some help to you."

"Ah," Clark says. "He wants to plead guilty."

Jerry holds up his hand. "You know better than that, Collier. What I mean is you've charged RoneCraft's Geoffrey Ross and Janice Steward in this matter as well. I'm certain we have some help for you there, especially since they're the top officers in the company. Nothing you can compel us to say, of course, given the Fifth Amendment, but serious help in seeing their charges through successfully. We could make a serious offer if things were right for my—for our—client."

"While that's intriguing, you're half admitting a role in all this. So it would seem we're on the right track pursuing your client."

"He was merely an employee who witnessed some things that you'd find interesting."

"I'm sure of that. So, he was involved?"

"Followed some orders, just like any other employee. But no, he didn't do what you allege."

"Maybe Steward and Ross say the same thing about him."
He nods toward Armstor, who has grown oddly calm and studies his fingernails as if merely soaking in the bathtub before bed.

"Careful who you believe," Jerry says.

"Okay, so what do you have in mind?"

"Drop the charges, and we'll cooperate fully."

"Now you're the one who should know better."

"What would convince you?"

"Give me something."

"Can't. Not without an idea of where it would take us."

"That's what I need to know—where it will take us."

Jerry smiles. We've reached the expected Mexican stand-off, guns drawn while both men wish they were on the other side of each other's facts. "Fair enough, for now," Jerry says. "Let us think about it. We all have to be downstairs in court in a few minutes anyway. But I hear you're willing to entertain..."

"I'm willing to listen to solid information. That's all I'll say."

It's hard to explain to the Armstors how the meeting advanced their cause. Still, Samuel didn't seem as interested as he should have been, and somewhere during the meeting, he stopped fidgeting and folded his hands on the table. Meghan, though, grew ever more edgy, although she didn't say a word.

I sit down in the late morning courtroom next to Jerry. I can tell my face is shiny again. Jerry still looks cool next to Armstor, who still seems not to care.

I notice the newly opened courtroom has been retrofitted with a century-old judge's bench and witness stand. The galley is separated by a low gated fence whose near-black varnish matches the bench. It was meant to add character but only looks out of place in the wash of modern fluorescence and the pale wallpaper. I get a strong sense of apathy from the place.

Armstor glances at me, then averts his eyes. They dart side

to side, and he finally turns to look at his wife. My eyes follow, and I see her sitting neatly just behind the defense table. I glimpse Margaret in the back of the room next to the door and nod. She nods back, her eyes fixed on me until I feel her probing again.

I watch as Armstor returns to the annoying cleaning of his fingernails, using the longest nail of his left pointer. I think about saying something, but he won't look up from his task. Ellen comes up behind us, and Jerry confers with her quietly.

I look across at the prosecution's table. Collier Clark doesn't acknowledge me, the bastard. His assistant, a young woman with short dark hair, looks amazingly like him, except she wears a dark skirt. I look at Jerry and Ellen, then back at Clark and his assistant.

They all look alike.

How could one tell them apart, who was on whose side? It amazes me how formless lawyers are, all morphed together into a single, unique race of clones. There's nothing to distinguish one from another, like bees in a hive to the untrained eye. I shake myself. Nonsense.

In the beginning, Clark had been cordial. But after two months, he began to ignore our calls. Jerry ended up getting the documents Justice had taken from RoneCraft, but only after three court orders and a threat from the judge to hold Clark in contempt. Still, the last request went unsatisfied when the judge ruled that the government had turned over everything pertinent to the case.

Since then, Clark and his team have refused to talk. It didn't make sense.

Jerry had puzzled over this, too, but decided that since it was Clark's first time as lead prosecutor, it might be inexperience showing through, and that would come down in our favor. Ellen was certain Clark had decided to ignore attempts to embarrass him; he probably cleared it with his boss. Then, oddly enough, he agreed to the discussion this morning, from which I took real hope of a deal even though nothing happened and no one offered anything concrete. But then, that's how lawyer meetings go, and it amazes me how we find such hope in them.

The door behind the bench swings open, and the bailiff says, "All rise." Judge Topicz storms into the room. He bangs his gavel and tells the reporter to announce the case. He fidgets with his glasses case, finally able to make his thick fingers extract wire-rimmed reading glasses. He perches them on the end of his nose and wraps the wires around his ears. The glasses look out of place on Topicz, who seems more like a dock worker than a judge. He's not particularly tall but has a broad chest, so broad as to seem unnatural. His head is square and tough with serious, seasoned creases. Still, he might be someone's grandfather. He brushes a thick hand over his thin, grey crew cut, then looks down at Collier Clark, his face sober.

"Mr. Clark, I understand you've something for us to consider before we begin."

Clark stands. "Well, your honor, it seems we must go forward with the trial."

Topicz looks at Clark and then at me. "You here to waste our time?"

"No, your honor," Clark says.

"Mr. Williamsen, are you in agreement with his assessment of the situation?"

Jerry stands while I fumble. "Your honor, I'm not certain what Mr. Clark was referring to, but we've been looking forward to our day in court to clear this matter up so our client can get back to his life," Jerry says.

"Save it, both of you. I'm not impressed by swordplay," Topicz says. "All right then. My calendar has its first opening in October. That's three months away. Any objections?"

"No, your honor," Jerry says.

"Ah, well, the government is in no hurry here, your honor. We could go later in the fall or even after the first of the year."

Jerry looks surprised, and while I am too, the fact that *he* lets it show makes me smile.

"Mr. Koch?"

"No objections here."

"Fine. Then, we'll set this to begin on January 10th. I read your pleas and assume they haven't changed, then."

"Not guilty," Jerry says.

"Of course." Topicz waves one arm in the air. "Next case." He slams his gavel once, and we make our way to the hallway.

Jerry catches up to Clark. "You didn't tell us you were willing to delay trial."

"You didn't say you wanted it earlier."

"We don't."

"Then we both win, at least on that count." His eyes engage with Samuel's momentarily, and it almost seems that both men smile. Meghan puts her hand on my sleeve, but I step away and wag my head slightly. She backs away. Jerry takes Armstor by the elbow, and the two go off down the hall while Meghan follows them. She looks back just as Margaret comes beside me.

Margaret takes the file from my hands. "Well, now you'll have more time—to prepare, that is."

I look down at her hair. It's meticulous and yet messy at the same time. She looks tired, as if some heavy burden weighs on her. "You did a good job with Mrs. Armstor. She looked just right. But I wonder about the schoolgirl stockings."

"It wasn't my choice or my counsel, Mr. Williamsen. But I hope it was an improvement."

"Of course, of course. She looked fine, and besides, this wasn't much of a court date anyway. I wonder what prompted Clark to delay trial?"

"Have you talked to Marge Smithson recently?"

"No, why?"

"You should. I ran into her at your house two weeks ago." I look surprised. "Oh, I didn't tell you that I visited Shirley?"

"No. And Marge was there?"

"Yes. And before we left, she pulled me aside and said that Mr. Clark had been talking with someone associated with the case. She didn't know who, but I gathered he was on to something substantial." She tucks the files under her arms and presses them to her chest like a schoolgirl. I notice her looking up at me as I stare down the hallway where the group had disappeared.

I feel myself nodding slightly as if I had a tick. "That's all she said?"

"She was going to call you. I guess she didn't, and I'm sorry I didn't say..."

I put one hand in the air. "It's all right, Margaret."

"But I feel, well, responsible. It might have helped you to talk with her before today."

"No. Today was a joke as far as I'm concerned."

I turn toward her and notice she looks confused. I want to leave, but instead, I wait.

She puts one hand on my arm at the elbow. "I know... I know you're under a great deal of pressure, especially since Shirley stopped the chemo treatments."

My eyes flare, and Margaret pauses and almost steps back. Her mouth opens before stepping close to me and touching my arm again. "You look... You look as if you didn't know."

I laugh to choke back the lump that forms in my throat. I shake my head. "No, I didn't. Sad, wouldn't you say?" Margaret doesn't offer an opinion. But she still looks at me, still touches my arm. "Sounds like I should go home, Margaret. If you'll excuse me..." I pull my arm from her grasp in a rough motion. I consider apologizing, but I have momentum now, down the hall and toward Shirley. I remember that Carol will be there but decide I'll just throw her out.

The house is quiet when I enter. Carol is at her post on the stool at the kitchen island. She holds a book in the air, too high, but compensates with an upturned head and down-turned eyes peering through her reading glasses. Her neck arcs like a snake. "That looks uncomfortable," I say.

She looks at me over her glasses. "Winston, what are you doing here? In the middle of the day? On a Monday? When did you come in?"

"You should be a prosecutor, Carol. All your interaction is constant interrogation."

She frowns. "Look, I'm just surprised, that's all."

"Shirley up?" I ask.

"She was. But she went back to bed after a small lunch."

I look at my watch. It's one-thirty. "Well, I want to talk to her."

"What you want," she says, "and what Shirley needs seldom line up, Winston."

I'm surprised by the anger that surges into my forehead. "Look!" I stop and close my eyes. "Carol. Here's the deal. Today, you will leave. I will take care of Shirley. I can do that. I know her med..."

"She stopped taking her meds, Winston."

"That's what I was about to say," I say. "You don't think I knew that?"

Carol regards me with the truth we both know. "Okay," she says. "Are you going to talk with her or just take up space?"

"That's none of your business. I don't answer to you."

"That's your problem, Winston. You don't answer to anyone. But someday you'll have to answer to G..."

"Don't start on the goddamn God stuff."

Carol purses her lips and regards me. "I'll leave. But you better change your attitude before you talk to Shirley, or so help me, Winston..."

She stops when I raise my hand. "I will." The sincerity of my voice surprises even me. Carol stands up, gathers her book and purse and starts for the door. She turns around before opening it, but just looks at me momentarily. She leaves.

I stand in the kitchen until I hear nothing but the hum of the refrigerator and my own breath rasping in my throat, the air passing over the thick summer mucus of the faint but growing allergies I never had as a younger man. All that's left is to talk with Shirley.

I sense the bedroom no longer holds the faint odor of sickness and medicine, the battle of antiseptic and stale breath. There never was any real smell here, I tell myself. It was just the aura of death and postponement in the air she would breathe in and out and in and out. But now that I know she's taking no medication, stopped all chemo treatments, there is something different in the smell of the room. Even her grey form on the grey bed in the grey comforter has a sharpness to its color, the delineation of her body, and she seems almost separate and distinct from her surroundings and grows more so as my eyes adjust to the light. And this distinctness of form is human and unique, its very own being, almost precious. Or, maybe I humanize what's left of her because that's what I need to see as life leaks out of her.

"Carol?"

"No, Shirley, it's me."

"Winston?"

Anger flashes up inside me again. She had to ask but wasn't sure. "Yes," I say as softly as I can.

She rolls over to face the door. I watch as her body moves together instead of in segments, rolling over in stages. She has more strength without the chemo, but the paradox is that she also draws closer to death and faster.

"What are you doing here? What time is it?"

"It's almost two in the afternoon." I move closer to the bed. "I talked with Margaret about the chemo. I didn't know."

"I never told you?"

"No, well, not that you were really going to do it. Stop taking it, I mean."

Shirley sighed. "And Carol?"

"She said nothing."

"Well, she's a bad girl." I'm surprised by how quickly she comes to. I say nothing. Shirley waits. Still, I say nothing. "And so what do you think?" she asks.

"I don't know what to think."

She laughs. "I've noticed that."

"Well, I mean, you were so miserable on the treatments that..."

"No, Winston. I mean, about yourself. You don't know what to think about yourself. It's all pretty clear to me what I have to do. But I worry about you."

"Me?"

"What will you do? When I'm gone, I mean."

"Shirley..."

"I know. I know about her. Oh, I'm sure you don't want to talk about her. Neither do I, really. But still, I worry what will become of you. I can't see you staying with the firm. But I can't see you anywhere else either. And as far as she's concerned, well, I expect that will be up to her, not you."

The matter-of-fact truth in her nonchalance makes her sound clinical. I struggle with what to say. She's never called me out in the open like this. I reach out with a feeble thought. "But you're my wife and..."

"Yes. And I'm convinced you'll not marry again. Unless, of course, she has a hold on you."

Shirley seems certain, confident even, with what she suspects or knows. "What do you know?" I ask.

"Nothing, really. Just that you're seeing a woman."

"Did Margaret..."

"No. Margaret is faithful to you and will be to the end, I believe. Besides, I respect her too much to ask, and she cares enough about us not to tell." I nod.

"Don't stand there like a puppy, Winston. I've decided I just don't have the time to dance around things anymore. I hope you can get used to it." I nod again. "I'm tired," she says, although I can't see it. "Let me sleep awhile longer. We can talk later." I nod and leave the room, hoping I can avoid later.

Chapter 11

Five days pass without my involvement in essentially anything important. Marge Smithson has been on my mind every day, but I don't call her. It's now Friday morning, and my only goal is to make it until evening when Paula will meet me at the Broadmore. But I can't wait. I leave the office early and make my way to the hotel, where I pick up the key from Stephen, who seems to have evolved to the lobby desk job from the bar. He smiles, and I stare at the bright red triangle of hair beneath his lower lip.

Shirley has worsened. She slept the whole week, and I could only visit her twice for a few minutes each time I looked in on her. I've essentially moved into the den myself. But today, the hospice nurse showed up for the first visit, something Carol insisted on.

When I open the door to the hotel room, a wave of loneliness sweeps over me. Paula had said she'd meet me by seven tonight. She'd gone to visit her father again and promised she'd come back and spend the weekend. This room and Paula seem like the only normal things left. I lie down on the bed and wonder what has brought me to define normality as meeting a mistress in a hotel room.

I look at the clock and worry about how to get through the day until she gets here. I pick up the TV controller but put it back down next to the phone. I stand up, walk to the window and study the cityscape. I could take stock.

Anyone who knows what I'm doing would be sickened, and at some level, I am sickened, too. But I can't help myself and, in fact, want so badly to see Paula and hold her and be with her even as Shirley's life ebbs away.

Maybe there's nothing good left anywhere now that Shirley is at death's door. I lie back down on the bed, then jump when the phone rings.

"Hello."

"Oh, uh, oh, Winston?"

"Paula? Is that you? Where are you? When do you think you'll get here?"

"Well, I, well, Winston. What are you doing there now?"

"I just couldn't stay home with the hospice nurse there and Carol."

"What about the office? I thought you'd be there."

"I couldn't face it. When are you getting here? I miss you." There is silence on the other end of the line. "Paula?"

I hear her breath in the receiver. "That's why I was calling."

"What do you mean? If you thought I'd be at the office, why didn't you try there?"

"Look, Winston. I'm not coming." She pauses. "I'm not coming at all. I'm moving back in with Daddy here in Cincinnati."

I pull the receiver down to my chest and put my free hand over my face. I put the receiver back to my ear. "Paula, when... when did you decide this? Why don't you want to see me? I mean, we've, well, we've been so close for so long that..."

"That's why I didn't want to talk to you in person. I just couldn't do it. I thought I could leave a message for you on the hotel phone. I didn't expect you to be there."

"But..."

"I know, it doesn't seem right. But *we're* not right, Winston, we're not right at all. You don't love me, you never have, and... and I can't go on kidding myself."

I hold the phone down again and feel weak. I lay back on

the bed and lifted the receiver. "Tell me, were you ever going to see me again? Or were you just going to leave a voicemail, and then I'd never hear from you again?"

I hear what sounds like crying on the other end of the line. "Paula?"

"I wasn't going to see you. I won't see you. Don't you see what a mess we are? You have a wife who's close to death. Your father's in the same place. Well, all we do by seeing each other is complicate everything more than it already is."

"But I thought you loved me."

"I thought so, too," she sobs. "But I don't, or even if I do, I shouldn't. Can't you see it's hopeless? I have a life ahead of me."

I sit up and look at myself in the vanity mirror. It's true. She does have a life, and from what she can see, mine's imploding. How could I expect her to be serious? I'm twenty-two years older than she, the same tattered old man I've dreaded becoming.

"Winston?"

I don't know why, but I laugh.

"Winston, are you all right?"

"Yes, oh, yes I am," I say and laugh again.

"What are you laughing about?"

"I just discovered that I agree with almost everyone I know..." I take a deep breath. "...that I'm not much good." I laugh full out, a loud and continuous laugh, until I feel tears.

"Winston, you're scaring me."

"Oh, don't be silly. See, I know it's taken me a while, nearly fifty-eight years. But I'm finally getting it. I finally understand what I am. Paula, don't you see? It's a relief, a huge relief to finally get it."

"I don't know what you mean."

"I know you don't, you couldn't. Hell, Paula, you're just a child." I laugh again. "Now, don't get angry." I can hear her breathing. "See, Paula, I'm letting you go. No, no, I'm *telling* you to go." I laugh again, then sober my voice. "It's okay. I'm okay.

You, Paula, you're going to be okay. You'll have a great life. Look, maybe it would have been different if we'd have moved to Paris, the left bank." I pause. "That's a joke. It's all right to laugh." I laugh, but she isn't laughing with me. "Okay, Paula, okay. This is the right thing. It's the right time." Without thinking, I say, "Goodbye."

"Goodbye, Winston. I hope...Well, I hope..."

"You..." The phone goes dead on the other end of the line. I leave the receiver off the hook. I pull the covers back, strip to my briefs, and slide under the sheets.

I open my eyes, and it takes me some time to understand the sun is close to setting. I've slept most of the day away. I feel as if I could sleep another day but have an urge to get up. The conversation with Paula comes back. I should call home. I should check on my father. So many things I should do—or should have done. This could be the moment—the one when I finally rise above myself. I look in the mirror by the door of the hotel room. That is me, isn't it?

Instead, I opt for the office because... no one will be there, and I can continue the hard work of avoidance.

I see Jerry's light on and, as quietly as I can, make my way to his door. When I peer in, I see him at his desk with a younger man standing behind him. They're looking over some papers.

"Excuse me," I say.

Jerry looks up. He wears a silk T-shirt, and his hair has waved itself to its natural attraction. There's little left that says he's a lawyer. He seems surprised but not overly so. "Oh, hi, Winston. Didn't know you'd be back. Where were you today? Margaret was looking for you?"

"I was out." I look at the young man beside him. He's taller than Jerry and probably at least a dozen years younger. While not really blonde, his tan is deep and makes him look blonde. He has a striped camp shirt on, and I can see his tanned legs beneath the strings of cut-off hiking shorts. I make him as the type I'd expect of Jerry.

Jerry notices. "Winston, this is Jason. Jason, Winston." We nod. "Jason is the executive manager at the Oakbrook Assisted Living Center." Jerry's eyes level on me, the casual demeanor disappears in an instant, and the attorney rises up in them. "I know this is a difficult topic for you, Winston, but we're moving your father in there tomorrow morning."

"Dad?"

"Yes. I wish we'd had a chance to talk, but well, you haven't been around much lately, have you? Your father has needed this for some time now, and Jason had an opening come up yesterday, so I took it. We're just now going over the financial arrangements." Jerry pauses, and I find myself nodding, lips pressed tightly together. "Would you like to see the facility?" he asks.

"No," I say, "I'm sure it's top-notch."

"You'll visit him, of course. He'll have his own apartment, and there'll be professional help on his wing twenty-four hours a day."

"Of course," I say.

"Jason here is really doing us a favor. Your father is probably beyond qualifying for assisted living, but Jason's willing to give it a try. If that doesn't work, then just next door is the nursing home, affiliated, of course."

I look at Jason. Beyond his physical attractions, his face has a boyish earnestness, do-gooder, I think. "So you'll be caring for my father." He comes around the desk with his hand outstretched.

"Yes. I mean our staff, of course. We have a great staff, Mr. Williamsen. Our organization prides itself on the concept of client dignity." I offer him a limp palm.

"So you've met him?" He shakes it firmly, then turns to Jerry, who nods.

"Yes, I have. We just came from his house. I've made arrangements for one of my staff to spend the night. We'll bring him to the facility in the morning."

"All at a cost, I imagine."

"We found him in the den," Jerry says. "He'd fouled himself and wet himself, and he was disoriented."

"Jerry, this is going to be hard enough for Winston..." Jason ventures.

"I know," Jerry replies. "But sometimes Winston needs to have things clearly spelled out. Your father, Winston, needs more than a day nurse, and he has for some time now."

"Well, I thought you were in charge. Expected so, in fact, and that's why I didn't check on him. So, you haven't been living up to your obligations? Too bad Dad can't understand that, or your power of attorney might be at risk."

"Okay, okay, I know. I should have been there sooner than I was. But whenever I went, he seemed in control. Only in the past couple of weeks has he slipped this far. Tonight, he hardly knew me."

"I know the feeling," I say.

Jason steps closer. "Mr. Williamsen, this is going to be very stressful. Let me assure you that he'll be fine now that we've connected with him."

I look at Jerry. "How much is this going to cost?"

"It's ten thousand a month. There's a lot included. Physical therapy, movies, meals..."

"I just wanted to know, that's all. I'm sure you've got him lined up with the best." I look at Jason again. He stands up.

"Okay, Winston, now I'm going to assert my authority here. He's your father, but I've got the legal responsibility for him, and I'm taking good care of him, and he can afford it. So you can relax or not. It won't matter to your father."

I sit down in the armchair at the back of Jerry's office. Jason's face is full of sympathy. I can see it comes from the bottom of his being, and I resent it. But more than that. I know from pathetic cases I've seen over the years that empathy, faked or otherwise, is so much better than sympathy. Sympathy will ultimately wear you down and overtake you. I conclude that Jason's tenure at caring for old people will not last. I look at Jerry and resent *him* even more. "So. Dad crosses over here," I say.

"Excuse me?" Jason says.

I cover my eyes for a moment. When I look up, I know they are red. I struggle with my words. "He's on the slide now. First, assisted living, then the nursing home, then into the obscurity of dementia that he'll never know he entered, never know he left."

"Our exercise and daily schedule will stimulate him. It'll give him the best chance to..."

I put up one hand and look at Jerry. "I'll never know, Jerry, how a woman genetically equipped to live past one hundred took an early out. Guess my mother was sick of my father."

Jerry nods in recognition. "Your mother was a great lady, Winston."

"Average. Average, I'd say. She had her faults. She put up with him, never confronted him except to tell him Shirley was good enough for me, something he never believed."

"Your father eventually came around on Shirley, Winston. We both know that."

I sigh. "You're right. Not that it matters now." Jerry sits down as I continue. "So now he disappears. Different parts of him at different times. I expect, if he were cogent, he'd admit seeking immortality in leaving everything to the University of Chicago."

Jason looks at both of us. "Let's not go there now. Winston here just needs some time, don't you?" Sadness pushes me to the brink of tears, and I struggle to find a way out. I don't reply.

Jerry stands up again and comes around his desk to stand beside Jason. He puts his arm around him. I notice, stare even. The look on his face is almost matter-of-fact. He smiles slightly, and it strikes me that the truth may be freeing us at this moment. I nod, hesitate, then say, "Seems like Jason will be good for Dad, Jerry."

"He will be, you'll see. It's the best care he can get."

Both men start to leave, Jerry with his arm still around Jason's shoulder. Something about that moves me. Before they close the door, I call out, "Jerry."

They turn around and step back into the office. "Yes?" he asks.

"I hope two are good for each other, too."

They smile. "Thank you, Winston," Jerry says. They pull the door shut behind them, and the thought of crying, just so recently overwhelming, leaves me.

Chapter 12

On Monday, I arrive late and sit in my office with the door closed. The phone rings through to my desk, so I know Margaret is passing it along. I hit the intercom. "Who is it?"

"A man. He said it would be the most important call of the day."

"His name?"

"He wouldn't tell me, but he said to mention wooden boats, and you'd know who it was."

I do, of course, but pretend otherwise. "Sounds like spy stuff," I say. "Do we represent any spies, Margaret?"

She almost laughs. "Not that I know of, sir. But if we did, I wouldn't be allowed to know about it, would I?"

"True, true," I say. "Okay, I'll take it. Just let it flash for a minute." I had half hoped it was Armstor because he's been acting strange and, with the delay of his trial, has told me to back off. He says Matt has assured him it's all covered. I suspect otherwise, or why would Matt be calling me?

"Hello, Matt," I say. "Been a while."

"Yes, Winston, and how are you?"

"I think you might be in a position to tell me. But I hope this isn't about more money. We covered that in May, and as far as I'm concerned, nothing's changed." I'm pleased by my tone, the fact I've got him in my sights.

"It might be about money, but not mine, Winston. Your friend Armstor is the one you should think about."

"And your meaning?"

"Look, we both know he's got more money. A pile of it somewhere. Based on our last meeting, I assume he's giving you some of it with a promise of a lot more, or you'd bale out on him."

"You can assume what you want."

"Fair enough, and I'll take that as a yes. Now, how well do you know him?"

"How well do we know anyone?" I like my sense of timing.

"Stop the bullshit, Winston. I'm doing you a favor."

"Really. And what might that be?"

"Okay, I'll just spit it out. Armstor has been meeting with your buddy at Justice. What's his name? Clark?" I sit back in my chair. Armstor's near smile with Clark after the hearing flashes in my mind. His lack of caring for what went on there. And yet, he'd been nervous...

"You still with me?" Matt finally asks.

"Yes," I say. "Why are you telling me this, and why should I believe you?"

"Why, you ask. Do you mean that, or is it just more of your philosophical bullshit? Look, I'm telling you, he's been working on a deal for himself. I know he's got more money, and I know they can't find it, not even that it's missing. He's helping Clark build a coffin for CEO Ross and CFO Steward. Trying to get himself a get-out-of-jail-free card in the process. I thought you'd like to know since I'm pretty sure he'll have enough wood to fashion one for you and me along the way. You met with me, you took money like I did. We're both screwed. Armstor is pure treachery, and we're collateral damage in saving his own skin."

The anger in his voice is credible. I feel my bowel lighten, and the room fairly spins, but I squeeze the receiver until I can concentrate. "If you're telling the truth, he's in over his head."

"Yeah? Why don't you ask his wife? I talked to her the other day. She said you wouldn't, by the way, and she knows something's up, too. She also believes he has lots more cash that she doesn't know about. So she's out there blazing around behind his back, trying to figure out what he's up to. I figure she's the one in over her head. I think Samuel's got this by the balls, and she's out of the picture."

I pause for a moment to take stock. Samuel's been putting me off, Meghan's been trying to see me, Clark postponed the trial, Jerry thinks we're all on the straight and narrow and Ellen's found nothing of any money outside of what he'd told us about. "All right," I say, "I guess I can play along with you, at least to find out what we're going to do."

"We? Ha. Listen, I'm out of here. Milwaukee isn't all that attractive, anyway. So I'm gone."

"And why, again, are you telling me?"

"I just don't like to be double-crossed."

"This from a man who demands more money than he's agreed to?"

"Call it honor among thieves. Or just die if you want to, asshole." He hangs up.

My office is silent except for a ringing in my ears and the echo of *asshole, asshole, asshole* circling around me. That term would apply, I agree. But now things line up too well. I should have picked up on all of this, but I have spent my time ignoring everything I can possibly ignore.

Margaret comes in and hands me an envelope. I recognize Meghan's handwriting. I look up at her. "She here?"

"She was." Margaret looks apologetic. "I said you weren't in. She was pretty upset and almost cried. But she's gone now."

I nod. "Good. You can go now, Margaret. Home, I mean. Take the day off with pay."

She looks at me strangely, her head tilting slightly to one side, her eyes narrowing. "It's all right," I say. "Just go."

She hands me another note. "Carol called, too. She says things aren't going well. She couldn't wake Shirley this morning. She called her oncologist and tried to get her admitted.

The doctor said to call hospice, that they'd have the pain medication but that Shirley would..."

"Was she upset?"

"No. Not as I could tell. She was very calm. It was almost frightening. Look, Mr. Williamsen, if you want me to, I'll call Mrs. Armstor. You..."

I shake my head. "I think you've just found another reason to go home, Margaret."

"But..."

"Go home. Take care of your husband. Surprise him. You know, for someone who's always followed orders so well, you're sure having a hard time with this one." She looks defeated.

"Margaret," I say, "if I were in a battle about to be overrun by the enemy, I'd want to be in your foxhole. But now's the time to retreat. Live to fight another day; discretion is the better part of valor. All that." I lean forward and grasp her forearm. "Trust me on this."

"I've always trusted you."

"I know. It's your only flaw," I say and force a laugh. "That's a joke. I would never do anything to..."

"I know that. That's why I trust you."

"Then trust me now. You don't want to be around for a while. I'll make sure Jennifer knows to back you up. She can just take the calls and stack them up. Most of what she'll get will be payments from deadbeats or sad letters about why they can't pay. We won't hear from anyone else after today." I can tell she finally gets it. She nods quickly several times.

"All right. Should I call Carol before..."

"No. Just go." Margaret looks at me one more time, takes her purse from her desk and leaves.

I pick up the envelope from Meghan and feel its weight, metaphorically, that is. Based on what Matt said, I know what's in it. Or, if I don't know, then it's not something I can deal with. Not now, at least. She's been betrayed, and she knows it and wants me to help fix it. I can't, and if I could, I wouldn't. There's been enough, enough for a lifetime.

I toss the envelope in the wastebasket without destroying it. Maybe someone will find it; maybe it'll go unnoticed. None of that matters to me anymore. I'll await the subpoena, or the suspension notice from the Bar Association, or the arrival of an arrest warrant complete with a couple of badged officers. Maybe all of the above.

The note is in Margaret's perfect script, yet I can hardly read it: "couldn't wake Shirley... oncologist... call hospice... pain..." Yes, pain.

On the way home, I decided that Jerry should know everything. But it can wait until tomorrow. He'll be shocked, or maybe not. Maybe just disappointed. I expect he'll look over our errors and omissions insurance and discover what he already knows: that it won't cover me or protect the firm from blatant wrongdoing. And Clark will likely file criminal charges against the firm and not just me.

When my father left the management to me, he never dreamed he'd set the firm on this course. But with nearly everything falling apart, I sense manifest destiny at work. Failure preordained. I've spent most of my life behind the façade of something I'm not. That false front has finally eroded enough to expose who I really am. Now, it will be made public. Knowledge shared with the world. Seated in history forever. I never set out to become this barren of both ethics and morals, but there it is, the false front of respectability offset by an equal and opposite force of deceit. If only it resulted in a zero-sum game. But it ends in the red, worse than if I'd never lived. Maybe Jerry can protect the firm.

Lawyering, it's all nonsense.

- - -

Shirley's bedroom is as quiet as the sanctuary my mother would sometimes take me to on Sunday nights when the only parishioners were wispy women kneeling on hard kneelers in St. Anthony's church. I stand just inside the door of the room and half wish for a candle to light.

Carol had greeted me at the door with a slight smile. She ushered me upstairs and took the hospice nurse back downstairs without a word. She was so quiet it seemed she was floating. I should be grateful but miss our normal insults since they had once served to toughen me for what I now see lying in our bed.

Shirley has on a new flannel nightgown. It's bright, multi-colored, and almost cheerful in the dusk of light that passes through the heavy shades drawn tight against the windows. I see movement, and it draws me closer.

"Winston?"

I hurry to the bedside. "Yes, it's me," I say. "Darling," I say.

She looks up, half smiles as her eyes focus on my face. "I'm glad you're here."

I sit beside her and take her hand. "Are you in pain?"

She musters a small laugh. "No. Not with the knock-out drops Carol just gave me." I look across the bed and see the IV in her arm.

"That's good," I say.

"That's one opinion," she says. We fall silent. Then, a dry cough. "Please," she whispers, "lie down beside me."

I maneuver myself down onto the bed. She's lying too close to the edge, and I lay on a narrow sliver of the mattress with one arm above my head. I grasp the headboard so I don't fall off.

"Comfy?" she asks.

"Yes, never been this comfortable."

"Good."

I let go of her hand and gently lay my arm across her stomach. She puts her palm on my forearm, and together, we lower its weight fully onto her. I feel her fingers sliding up and down my arm in a narrow range. I close my eyes and concentrate on breathing as vitreous floaters pass across my pupils like stars in a microcosmic sky.

My stomach is calm. I search for the sense of dread I know so well, but it's gone. In a moment, I'm sure she's asleep, but her fingers keep moving. I try to slide further onto the bed, and her fingers stop at my motion. So, I hold myself perfectly still.

Soon, they move again, gently, up and down my forearm, as if picking up where they left off.

About Atmosphere Press

Founded in 2015, Atmosphere Press was built on the principles of Honesty, Transparency, Professionalism, Kindness, and Making Your Book Awesome. As an ethical and author-friendly hybrid press, we stay true to that founding mission today.

If you're a reader, enter our giveaway for a free book here:

SCAN TO ENTER
BOOK GIVEAWAY

If you're a writer, submit your manuscript for consideration here:

SCAN TO SUBMIT
MANUSCRIPT

And always feel free to visit Atmosphere Press and our authors online at atmospherepress.com. See you there soon!

About the Author

Rodney Nelsestuen has published more than a dozen works of fiction and nonfiction in a variety of literary journals. In addition, his writing has won or been honored in a number of literary contests. He's frequently served as a judge in several writing contests including the Minnesota Book Awards, the Pacific Northwest Writers' Association, and the national Eric Hoffer Award. He has written professionally on financial services and technology. Rod holds an MFA from Hamline University in St. Paul, Minnesota, and has previously taught at The Loft Literary Center in Minneapolis.